THE
POLICY
PARTNERSHIP

Presidential Elections and
American Democracy

Bruce Buchanan

ROUTLEDGE
NEW YORK AND LONDON

Published in 2004 by
RoutledgeFalmer
29 W 35th Street
New York, NY 10001
www.routledge-ny.com

Published in Great Britain by
RoutledgeFalmer
11 New Fetter Lane
London EC4P 4EE
www.routledge.co.uk

RoutledgeFalmer is an imprint of the Taylor & Francis Group.

Printed in the United States of America on acid-free paper.

10 9 8 7 6 5 4 3 2 1

Library of Congress Cataloging-in-Publication Data for this book is available from the Library of Congress

Table of Contents

Preface

Democracy and Policy

The presidency was neither designed nor expected to act in concert with the American people. The Framers intended Congress to represent and express the popular will, but those intentions were dashed, and the presidency democratized, by disputes over policy. Thomas Jefferson and Andrew Jackson, moved by widespread public outrage at perceived abuses of power, led mass movements that captured the executive and legislative branches and as a result forced major changes in the presidency, electoral politics, and national policy.

These developments also spawned a new and different kind of relationship between the presidency and the people. Born of anger, rooted in policy, formalized by elections, the relationship dates to 1800 but has been extended and elaborated in fits and starts, and in ways large and small, ever since. The upshot is that contemporary presidents — still the only nationally elected officials charged with protecting the broadest public interest — can credibly echo Andrew Jackson's original claim to be the direct representative of the people.

The popular link behind that claim not only greatly increased the power of the presidency, as is often pointed out; it also increased the potential for popular influence. Ordinary citizens would, from time to time, have reason to think of themselves as partners in joint ventures with presidents and therefore entitled to some voice in setting the direction of national policy. Nor are the prospects for popular influence entirely reliant on the voluntary beneficence of particular presidents. The electoral system gives voters the leverage to influence policy. The need for votes forces candidates to respond when public expectations are clear. That creates opportunities for policy understandings: election to office in return for responsiveness to voter concerns. In the theory of democracy, elections exist precisely to give citizens the means to compel leaders to accommodate their interests. Those interests are served or thwarted by what government does or does not do, which is a good working definition of *policy*. If voters cannot influence what government does, then what is the point of democracy? That is why, in the end, the central questions of democratic politics come down to the relationship between popular electoral choices and public policy (Ginsberg 1976, 41).

In the real world of contemporary political practice, however, the design increasingly leaks around the joints, diluting if not trumping the prospects for citizen influence. Presidential candidates treat elections as power struggles, not as debates on the issues, and that frequently clouds the policy implications of electoral choices. The fixed four-year presidential term of office creates delays in accountability and gives presidents freedom to act with limited fear of electoral reprisal for broken campaign promises or unpopular decisions. The mass public rarely unites to demand presidential attention to clear majority policy agendas. Much of the time, people are content to simply defer to the policy guidance and leadership offered by the president and other leaders (Brody 1991; Zaller 1992). To make matters worse, many potential voters are losing interest. The decline of voter turnout in presidential elections since 1960 signals a growing public indifference. As turnout has dropped, feelings of political obligation and citizen duty have waned. Meanwhile, elected officials have grown more assertive. Researchers now find evidence of "a decline in democratic responsiveness at the very top of American national government" (Shapiro and Jacobs 2000, 2), and of elite dominance so pervasive that the very idea of public influence on policy seems largely mythical (Dye 2001).

These developments suggest the need for taking stock. What has become of the policy relationship potential created by presidential elections? To what degree do contemporary candidates and presidents take into account voter policy wishes before and after elections? What is the nature and extent of the influence that voter participation can have on policy? What are the prospects for reversing the trends — increased citizen indifference and decreased elite responsiveness — that diminish the chances for policy partnerships? These are the questions addressed in this book.

My interest in such questions was inspired by the historic democratization of the presidency that I just touched on, and by the idea of a special reciprocal relationship between citizens and presidents that is sometimes associated with it (Buchanan 1987). My interest was reinforced by an involvement in three large-scale studies of candidate, media, and voter interactions during the 1988, 1992, and 1996 presidential election campaigns, all sponsored by the John and Mary R. Markle Foundation. The results of that research forcefully demonstrated the large gap between ideal and reality in presidential politics and the very limited prospects for improvement (Buchanan 1991; 1996; 2004). That made me a realist. But I am still of the opinion that presidents and citizens can and should come to terms, at least on the big questions, before policy is enacted. In the old dispute over whether democracy wants voters to help set policy or simply to judge the results of policies set by their representatives, I lean toward the former. I will make no argument here for utopian transformations, for naïvely unrealistic levels of civic activism, or for a return to some golden age that never really existed. But I continue to believe that the tradition behind the presidency-public relationship, as well as the imperatives of good stewardship at the political system level, invites a continuous effort to improve the health of the policy relationship at the center of the world's most visible representative democracy. That is why it is important to ask what it would take to foster something even just a little bit better than a strictly minimalist, "Schumpeterian" version of representative democracy at the presidential level in America. I use the six chapters that make up this book to work toward that goal.

The Plan of the Book

The "something better" that is worth seeking is a situation in which presidents and citizens more often reach agreement on the most important national problems and their solutions before policy is enacted. Such agreement is made possible by the incentives created by elections. Before asking how to achieve more, however, we must first study how much and what kind of voter policy influence there is now. Chapter 1 examines key characteristics of the twelve presidential elections between 1956 and 2000, and it uncovers evidence showing that election-related citizen influence on national policy, although very limited, does in fact exist. What is more, close examination of case histories shows that it takes different forms in different elections, depending on the dispositions of the candidates and the state of the voters in varying political circumstances. This prompted the typology that is sketched with statistics, charts, and brief examples in the opening chapter and fleshed out with more elaborate case analyses in the three chapters that follow, each of which explicates a different kind of voter policy influence.

Chapter 2 offers examples of *direct influence,* which arises when majorities know what they want and make clear to elected officials that they expect to get it quickly. Chapter 3 examines what I call *anticipatory influence,* which is exerted when candidates and/or presidents let their own expectations of how voters might react influence their choices of proposals and policies. Chapter 4 details examples of *legitimizing influence,* which voters may enjoy when candidates and/or newly elected presidents believe that they cannot hope to succeed in Congress without public endorsement of their proposals.

My explication of the varieties of voter policy influence through an examination of cases is an important part of what I have to offer, but the purpose of this book is not just to sketch a typology. The typology is actually a means to another end: clarifying the options for increasing voter leverage.

If constitutional change is ruled out (I do not propose it here), then increasing voter policy influence necessarily means strengthening the existing sources. As we will see, the potentials for enhancement vary. For example, anticipatory influence, though it will remain a necessary part of the citizen influence equation, by its nature cannot be strengthened. Unlike the other types, it makes no demands on voters (that is, it requires no prior voter learning, nor consensus on policy, nor any particular show of participatory zeal). For that reason, it is best understood as democracy's "default option." As such, it is a valuable constraint on leaders. By itself, however, it can yield no more than the Schumpeterian minimum — influence that must rely exclusively on politicians' fear of expected electoral reprisal to be effective. Because no prior consultation of voters' *actual* as opposed to their *imagined* policy preferences is required, there is no built-in need to come to terms with voters on policy before it is enacted.

Direct voter policy influence, on the other hand, most closely approximates the democratic ideal of ensuring voter input on policy before it is enacted, but it is also rare and difficult to achieve. As the cases in Chapter 2 will suggest, it usually emerges only in response to crises. To make it a regular noncrisis feature of the voters' civic portfolio would require special effort. The surest way to do it is long and hard: instill in a new generation more proactive and aggressive ideas about the meaning of civic duty (Buchanan 2004). Legitimizing influence has more immediate promise, as it emerges from a relationship between presidents and publics that can be forged during election campaigns (see Chapter 4), but it too is rare as well as highly unpredictable. To make it less so would require something other than a program of citizen education.

What I propose, then, is a way to strengthen both direct and legitimizing influence by combining them and making them less dependent on chance or circumstance. My proposed method involves reviving and updating the idea of the policy partnership. This, too, is a difficult option; neither a quick fix nor a panacea. Given the limits imposed by the structure of the American electoral system and by the incentives of presidents and publics, however, there is no better way in the near term to strengthen the public hand.

Of course, that which strengthens voters may weaken presidents, prompting the latter to resist. Why, for example, should presidential candidates risk staking out potentially controversial policy positions and asking voters to endorse them when it is often easier to get elected by downplaying or sidestepping policy? And why should new presidents bother to invoke the support of the people for their agendas when what really counts are the votes in Congress, which can often be had without a show of popular support? The last three presidents to run on big, clear policy agendas — Lyndon Johnson, Ronald Reagan, and the second George Bush (whose cases are reviewed in Chapter 4) suggest some answers.

Each of these leaders ran on a substantive platform, and after the election each invoked his victory and its implication of voter policy endorsement as leverage in Congress. Each claimed, in other words, to have achieved a policy mandate from the American people. Their claims show what partnerships can give presidents — *political leverage* — and also what can be in it for voters — a form of *recognition and policy influence* — that is the most voters can hope to achieve outside of crisis circumstances.

This potential for mutual benefit is what makes it more feasible here than elsewhere to ask how to expand the voters' share of influence. It invites a search for the lessons of these three "claimed consent" cases and other recent political experiments (most notably that of Ross Perot in 1992) to pull together the elements of a plan for the future.

In Chapter 5, therefore, I examine the preconditions for successful policy partnerships. The core of the partnership idea is presidents campaigning on an agenda and asking the electorate to mandate the agenda with their votes. Because so few presidents have been willing to try this, however, outside help is needed to nudge them along. I propose new agents and actions that can generate voter consensus on top policy problems and motivate candidates and presidents to offer solutions. To make this happen requires the orchestration of direct influence.

Late in Chapter 5 and more extensively at the end of Chapter 6, I use political fiction to show how my plan can work. Fictional candidates are pressured to suggest and debate long-term solutions to real-world problems they would have preferred to avoid: the viability of Social Security and the accessibility and affordability of health care. Here is where my proactive vision of the policy partnership is most clearly illustrated.

Such speculation necessarily takes us well beyond the case histories in Chapter 4, because nothing fully like what I have in mind has yet occurred. The real presidents who sought policy understandings with voters offer a prototype. Would-be reformers can use this prototype to construct possible futures, as I do. But only the presidents and electorates to come can truly extend the limits of the possible.

Chapter 1
A Typology of Voter Influence

Presidential elections are rich with implications for democracy in America. Not only do they permit the selection and retention of the peoples' choice for president, they also allow the public to express its policy preferences. While modern electoral studies have much to say about presidential selection, they have very little to say about the impact of the vote on policy. If the *raison d'être* of democracy is to permit ordinary citizens to influence what government does, then that is a serious oversight. The policy questions that most affect voter interests usually arise and are sometimes vigorously debated during presidential campaigns, but do those who take the trouble to vote in presidential elections actually influence policy?

Realignment theorists (e.g., Burnham 1970; Key 1955; Schattschneider 1960; Sundquist 1983) — that is, the people who study the shifting patterns of voter party allegiance throughout American history — are convinced that, in some cases at least, voters *do* influence policy. These theorists argue that all major shifts in partisan support set new directions for national policy. Indeed, the most widely recognized realigning elections — 1800, 1824, 1860, 1896, and 1932 — are all associated with passionate issue debates resolved by decisive presidential votes. Other critical elections of the distant past had clear policy consequences as well. For example, the 1864 election had almost as much impact on the fate of slavery and the shape of the postwar Union as the outcome of the Civil War itself (Waugh 1997).

As this example suggests, presidential elections that occur during national crises invariably feature debates about how to resolve those crises. The major political parties and their presidential candidates become associated with sharply different proposals, and voters settle the argument in ways that may also alter the balance of partisan power (Campbell et al.

1

1960, 74–76). Seen this way, it is policy that drives politics, not the other way around. That is, partisan realignments are politically significant mainly because they are brought about by shifts in voters' policy preferences (Chubb and Peterson 1985, 3–25). In such cases, voters help to set policy because they exercise their influence *before* policy is adopted.

Some empirical evidence exists (e.g., Ginsberg 1976) to support the realignment theorists' contention that several crisis elections in the distant past did actually force changes in policy, but most of the small store of interesting and relevant empirical research has been published more recently. A study by Patricia H. Conley (2001), for example, presents evidence in support of the argument that presidential elections do serve as signals of the popular will, and that the interpretation of election outcomes has a significant impact on policy change. The "mandate" is conceptualized as the perceived probability that voters will side with the president's policy views in the next election. The hypothesis is that, when this probability is high, legislators will accommodate presidential proposals; when it is low, they will resist. Examining data from the forty-three elections between 1828 and 1996, Conley finds that presidents tend to claim mandates when such factors as their percentage of the electoral vote and the number of the president's partisans in Congress encourage it. When these factors are marginal, mandate claims depend on the level of agreement between the executive and legislative branches. If agreement is within reach, a "bargained" mandate is possible. When agreement is improbable, presidents do not declare mandates.

As noted, Conley's model focuses on the "preferences and perceptions of the politicians who must set the policy agenda" (2001, 22). American politicians will respond to what the people want; since what they want is rarely perfectly clear, however, voter influence is almost always based on perceptions and assumptions, cued by fairly standard indicators (e.g., margin of presidential victory, degree of policy emphasis in the campaign, the clarity of policy differences between the winner and the loser, policy and partisan support for the winner in Congress, the characteristics of newly elected members of Congress, etc.). Perceptually filtered voter influence is indirect but still potentially significant. If members of Congress think the people have spoken in support of a president's agenda, they are much more likely to support it. It is not surprising, therefore, that Conley finds that presidents who score well on these variables experience greater legislative success, at least during their first year in office (2001, 74–75). Voter policy preferences therefore matter, especially when they are expressed through elections, "the major and most pertinent opportunity for politicians to take the pulse of the electorate" (Conley 2001, 14).

Another recent study makes the point that the size of the election victory also influences the policy ambitions of the victor. Ragsdale and Rusk (1999, 98) find, for presidents between 1953 and 1996, that the larger the margin of victory, the greater the number of positions presidents take on legislation before Congress. Put another way, the larger the victory, the greater the tendency to seek to influence and share credit for legislation. Ragsdale and Rusk also find, however, that when all Congressional roll-call votes on which the president has taken a position are included in the analysis (i.e., not just first-year votes), the greater the margin of electoral victory, the *lower* the success rate on Capitol Hill. They conclude that "while major electoral victories increase presidents' legislative activity, they do not translate into legislative success" (1999, 110). This is undoubtedly because high-margin victors take so many more positions on roll-call votes. The greater the number of positions taken, after all, the more opportunities there are for defeat. Ragsdale and Rusk imply as much when they say, "[n]ot unexpectedly, the longer the president has been in office, the lower his success rate."

Taken together, the studies conducted by Ragsdale and Rusk and by Conley show not only how empowering to presidents is the sense that they have the people behind them, but also how important it is, from the president's perspective, to strike while the iron is hot. Lyndon Johnson said it best: "You've got to give it all you can that first year. Doesn't matter what kind of majority you come in with. You've got just one year when they treat you right and before they start worrying about themselves" (quoted in McPherson 1972, 268).

A final strand of relevant scholarship uses an ever-expanding body of survey research to probe the extent to which public opinion can be shown to influence elite policy choice in general, with no special emphasis on isolating the influence uniquely attributable to elections. The major synthesis of this entire body of research shows a significant cross-time relationship between voter policy preferences on the one hand, and the policy actions of elected officials on the other (Page and Shapiro 1992). The most recent summary of the latest research, however, concludes, as noted in the Preface, that while public opinion was quite influential in the past, it has been decidedly less influential of late, with current evidence showing that the mass public's influence on policy has declined sharply (Shapiro and Jacobs 2000; Jacobs and Shapiro 2000).

Obviously, the available research evidence is neither abundant nor conclusive. Still, the studies yield an interesting mix of results. There is past evidence of voter policy influence, but this influence is in decline. Presidents are empowered by evidence of popular support, but its policy value to them may be short lived. The studies also reflect a truism that, for the purposes of this book, is well worth making explicit: the chances for voter influence on national policy are highly dependent on presidential agency. Voters have few other ways to affect what the national government does except through the efforts of presidents. To be sure, there are times when one party or coalition in Congress may be more responsive to a major part of the electorate than is a president, but it will always be easier for voters to forge policy understandings with a single chief executive who has campaigned on an agenda and established a relationship with the electorate than it is to do so with aggregations like parties or coalitions. Typically, it is the president, the only nationally elected official, and thus the most plausible spokesperson for the electorate as a whole, who deals with the relevant groups in and outside Congress. As a practical matter, therefore, if voters are to have much influence, they need presidents. Presidents also need voters, however, both to get elected in the first place and to add democratic legitimacy to their policy claims in the aftermath of Election Day. That gives voters real leverage, especially right before and right after elections. The question is whether — and, if so, how — voters actually use that leverage. The uncertainty surrounding how to gauge the will of the people makes it an open question as to whether presidents are responding to or manufacturing the popular will at any given time. That is why so many surrogate indicators of public preferences are used. Murky and uncertain though the contract may often be, however, there is an undeniable potential for reciprocity, a policy partnership, built into the electoral connection between presidents and the people.

The project described here began as an effort to clarify the nature of that potential. It does so by examining the metrics and qualities of a broad spectrum of recent elections to sort out and describe how the president–public policy interaction works now. The aim is to identify, define, and better understand the voter policy influence created by presidential elections. The project begins with numbers but ultimately does not rest on them. As we will see, it soon becomes necessary to move beyond the numbers to a more qualitative interpretation of actual cases. The following discussion offers an overview of both the quantitative and qualitative findings that prompted a typology of influence. Subsequent chapters flesh out most of the case particulars and justify the typology.

The Quantitative Project

Scope and Limits

The evidence is drawn from the twelve presidential elections between 1956 and 2000. Why this sample of elections? Because the defining features of contemporary American presidential politics came on line during this period: the emergence of television as a campaign tool, the diminished influence of party leaders in presidential nominations, the rise of candidate-centered presidential campaigning, and an historic decline in voter turnout in presidential elections. Not incidentally, this time period also features reliable Gallup Poll data on the issue priorities of voters just before elections — a key measure for our purposes — that were less readily accessible before 1956.

Theoretical Start-Point: Policy Consensus and Turnout

How should we approach the search for influence within these cases? By starting with what we know. It is obvious, for example, that citizens would have little or no policy influence at all if it weren't for elections. What is it about an election that makes such influence possible? It is the fact that elective offices are won with votes. Office and reelection seekers are therefore dependent on citizens because citizens control the votes. That dependency creates the potential for voter policy influence.

The next point, however, is this: elections do not make voter policy influence inevitable, only possible. The magnitude and the nature of such influence will vary with, among other things, the concessions citizens manage to extract from office seekers in return for their votes. Most office seekers will strive to minimize concessions in order to maximize their freedom of action. Therefore, candidate responsiveness to citizen-voters is likely to depend on candidate perceptions of the clarity and scope of citizen demands and the political costs of ignoring those demands. When candidates believe that enough prospective voters agree on what they want (e.g., polls say a majority wants a particular problem addressed) and that voters seem highly motivated to get what they want (as might be indicated, for example, by greater-than-usual prospective or actual turnout), voters are more likely to be influential than when there is no apparent consensus about the top problem (i.e., fragmented or conflicted public opinion) and little apparent concern about what is at stake in the election (with a projected or actual low turnout).

To put it more succinctly, our start-point is the proposition that voter policy influence is likely to be contingent on the levels of voter problem consensus and voter turnout. The greater the number of voters who agree that a particular problem requires elite attention, and the higher the level of voter participation (and/or any other indicator of the intensity of voter concern that may be available and be taken seriously by elites in context), the more likely are candidates or newly elected presidents to take voter preferences into account in deciding what problems to address, what solutions to propose, and, if elected, what to do.

Data

To test this proposition, we begin by juxtaposing two sets of empirical evidence: "the most important problem facing the nation," identified by the largest percentage of voters just before the election, on the one hand, and voter turnout on the other. This is done for each of the twelve elections since 1956. The percentages are shown in Table 1.1.

The "most important problem" data provides a measure of the salience of a particular issue or issue-set to the public; that is, how important does the public think the issue is. It does *not* measure what the public wants

TABLE 1.1 Voter Participation and Policy Consensus, 1956–2000

	Voter Participation[a]% Voting Age Population	Top Policy Problem	% Supporting Top Policy Problem[b]
1956	59.4	War Threat/Suez/Foreign Policy	48
1960	63.06	Build Bomb Shelters "Overwhelming majority says Russian relations the primary problem"[d]	71
1964	61.92	International/Cold War Problems	46
1968	60.84	Vietnam	51
1972	55.21	Vietnam	27
		Inflation/Cost of Living	27
1976	53.55	High Cost of Living	47
1980	52.56	High Cost of Living/Inflation	60
1984	53.11	Threat of War/International Tensions	30
1988	50.11	Budget Deficit	23
1992	55.09	Economy/Jobs/Deficit	81
1996	49.08	Economy/Jobs/Deficit	34
2000	51.2[c]	Education	18[e]

[a] *Source*: Federal Election Commission, unless otherwise indicated.
[b] *Source*: Gallup Polls, 1956–2000, unless otherwise indicated. Latest available pre-election survey dates vary from year to year.
[c] *Source*: Curtis Gans, Committee for the Study of the American Electorate.
[d] *Source*: Gallup, 1972: 1676. Gallup did not report specific number. Bomb shelter number included as a surrogate.
[e] *Source*: *Fox News*/Opinion Dynamics Poll, November 1–2, 2000.

done about the issue, a separate question that will be addressed when relevant in later case discussions. For present purposes, we represent the "most important problem" percentages as a reasonable indicator of the extent of voter demand that the government formulate a policy to address a particular issue or problem.

How should we interpret the demand numbers in Table 1.1? Note that they are based on the coding categories chosen and reported by Gallup analysts in their summary publications (e.g., Gallup 1972). Sometimes Gallup coders lump related issue concerns together into one omnibus measure. In 1992 and 1996, for example, that measure was "Economy/Jobs/Deficit." As Gallup "year in review" essays included with the poll results in their publications make clear, such combinations reflect considered judgments that, while different respondents emphasized different specific dimensions of the problem, the underlying economic unity was widely recognized and acknowledged in the political discourse of the time. Thus, while some 1992 observers may have seen "creating new jobs" and "fixing the deficit" as different and even competing problems, many influential economists then and now see them as compatible and closely related. For example, one prominent argument is that to reduce the federal budget deficit is to lower long-term interest rates. That in turn reduces the cost of capital, stimulating both productive investment and job creation. Influenced by such economic thinking, candidates and media then and now often treat such specifics as "jobs" and "the deficit" as constituent parts of a family of closely related economic problems. What is more, the linkage was and is sometimes recognized by the poll respondents. It therefore seems reasonable to interpret the 81 percent figure for 1992, for example, as indicative of widespread public demand that the government give economic problems priority attention.

As noted earlier, *voter turnout* is sometimes interpreted as a measure of the strength of voter interest and/or concern for the issues at stake in particular elections, and we use it that way here. If a national problem can be shown to have sparked mass anxiety in context, and if turnout increases significantly in the same year that policy consensus increases, then elevated turnout may well be a consequence and thus a plausible indicator of elevated policy concern. Figure 1.1, which uses the numbers in Table 1.1 to plot the cross-time (1956–2000) relationship between problem consensus and voter turnout, helps to make this point. The figure shows that problem consensus is much more volatile than turnout, and it was much more often lower (nine times) than higher (three times) in the past twelve elections. In two of those higher cases, 1960 and 1992, an increase in problem consensus *was* accompanied by an increase in turnout. Did the mass concern with problems increase turnout in those cases? In Chapter 2 we argue that the answer was "yes." Both years featured widespread voter policy anxiety, as well as other turnout drivers (a close and exciting race in 1960; and the salesmanship of Texas billionaire H. Ross Perot in 1992). Why did turnout decline slightly in the third example of an elevated problem consensus, 1980? My suspicion, explained in Chapter 4, is that the anxiety sparked by the cost of living and inflation was real, but its impact on turnout was mitigated by campaign-season ambivalence toward Ronald Reagan and his controversial economic proposals.

PT Index Construction

If our start-point proposition is correct, we should find that voters have the most policy influence when the combination of policy problem consensus and turnout is at its highest. Testing this expectation requires that

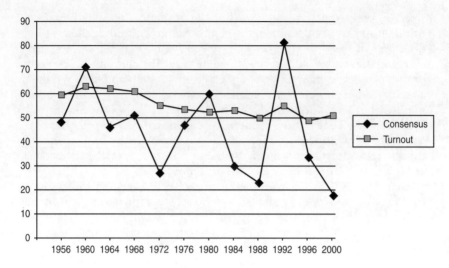

Figure 1.1 Policy Consensus and Voter Turnout 1956–2000

we rank the elections in these terms. Table 1.2 presents combined problem consensus and turnout (PT) rankings for the sample of twelve elections.

To see how the PT rankings are derived, consider the example of 1960. As Table 1.2 shows, it is the top-ranked turnout election and the second-ranked election in terms of the magnitude of the policy problem consensus measured by Gallup. That yields a combined average rank of 1.5 (1+2 = 3/2 = 1.5), which makes 1960 the top-ranked election on the PT index.

Analysis

Our strategy for isolating the difference that policy consensus and turnout make for voter policy influence is to maximize the PT variance by comparing only the lowest and highest cases on the PT scale. Whatever the influence variance in the middle-range cases might be, if our proposition is true we should find maximum influence in the highest PT cases and minimum or no influence in the lowest.

The two most highly ranked elections in Table 1.2 are 1960 and 1992. The two lowest are 1988 and 1996. The election of 2000, tied for last place with 1988, is for various reasons a special case and is taken up in detail in Chapter 4.

Do the highest PT elections generate more voter policy influence than the lowest? To answer this question, we must first identify a scheme for measuring influence. I argue that the influence attributable to electoral participation is best measured by the extent to which significant policy action that closely follows an election can be plausibly linked to voter priorities recorded just before the election. Relevant evidence is shown in

TABLE 1.2 Ranking of Elections by Policy Consensus and Turnout

	VOTER TURNOUT			POLICY CONSENSUS			PT INDEX	
	%	Rank		%	Rank		PT Means	Final PT Rank
1960	62.8	1	1992	81	1	1960	1.5	1
1964	61.9	2	1960	71	2	1992	3	2
1968	60.9	3	1980	60	3	1968	3.5	3
1956	59.3	4	1968	51	4	1956	4.5	4
1992	55.9	5	1956	48	5	1964	4.5	4
1972	55.2	6	1976	47	6	1980	5	5
1980	54.0	7	1964	46	7	1976	7	6
1976	53.5	8	1996	34	8	1972	8	7
1984	53.1	9	1984	30	9	1984	9	8
2000	51.2	10	1972	27	10	1996	10	9
1988	50.2	11	1988	23	11	1988	11	10
1996	49.0	12	2000	18	12	2000	11	10

Policy consensus: Percentage of respondents identifying a most important problem. Combined rankings: average of turnout rank and policy consensus rank.

Source: Voter turnout: Federal Election Commission.

Table 1.3, which compares the major postelection policy action of the two highest PT elections — 1960 and 1992 — to the two lowest — 1988 and 1996.

For each year, the major pieces of postelection legislative or other action most closely related to the top pre-election voter priorities are identified. Also included are other significant policy initiatives intended to characterize but not exhaust the important policy action of the ensuing presidency. I limit the lists to what might be called "high" policy, that is, a small handful of policy actions clearly among the most important of each presidency. Table footnotes identify the candidates' treatment of each issue and its postelection fate. These footnotes show that many policies that have not attracted strong voter interest get debated, and some are voted into law, as we would expect. The question here is, when majorities signal their problem priorities, do they get action?

Results

The evidence in Table 1.3 offers inferential support for the preliminary hypothesis. What we see, therefore, is that there is policy action on the majority voter priorities (indicated by an asterisk) after the election in the

TABLE 1.3 Postelection National Government Policy Action in the 1960, 1988, 1992, and 1996 Presidential Elections

1988	1992
Flag burning amendment[a]	1993 Deficit reduction budget[b] *
Capital gains tax cut[c]	Economic foreign policy[d]
1990 Budget agreement, savings & loan bailout, clean air act, and Gulf War [e]	Earned Income Tax credit[d]
	Health care reform[c]
Cold War steward[b]	Welfare reform[b]

1996	1960
1997 Balanced budget deal[e]	Increased defense spending[b] *
Entitlement reform[a]	Increased nuclear capability[b] *
Kosovo action[d]	Increased foreign and military aid[b] *
Education spending[d]	1963 Tax cut proposal[e]
	1963 Civil Rights proposal[d]
	Initial Vietnam commitment[d]

[a] Policy not discussed in campaign; introduced but not adopted.
[b] Policy discussed in campaign and adopted.
[c] Policy discussed in campaign but not adopted.
[d] Policy implied in campaign and adopted.
[e] Policy not discussed in campaign but adopted.
* Policy action related to voter priorities.

high PT cases. In the low PT cases, there are no majority voter priorities to begin with and, with one exception, no policy action on the top voter pluralities in either 1988 or 1996. The exception involves the potential link between the 23 percent plurality of voters that put the budget deficit on top of the rankings in 1988 (Table 1.1) and the budget deal of 1990 (Table 1.3). This exception is worth explaining because it shows why knowledge of case details is necessary to make sense of the numbers.

As a candidate in 1988, the eventual winner, George H.W. Bush, had advanced a "flexible freeze" on spending as a partial answer to the budget deficit. Then, in 1990, he initiated a budget deal with congressional Democrats aimed at reducing the deficit. Case histories presented in Chapter 2 support a claim that the policies that emerged in the high PT cases of 1960 and 1992 did so because the policy moves of new presidents — John F. Kennedy and Bill Clinton — were driven at least in part by a wish to respond to widespread public expectations. Bush's 1990 budget deal, however, was not a response to public demand. As the 1988 case discussion in Chapter 3 shows, Bush and his opponent, Massachusetts Governor Michael Dukakis, avoided any sustained discussion of the budget issue precisely because the expression of public concern for the problem was so low. Thus, by campaign's end, only 36 percent of a national sample of prospective voters was even aware that Bush had made a proposal that dealt with the budget deficit (Buchanan 2004, 88).

If Bush was not responding to public pressure, Kennedy and Clinton were, which should not be surprising. Why wouldn't voter influence be at its peak when a majority of voters signals problem-solving expectations that might eventually be enforced at the polls? Politicians have every reason to respond to clear voter demand backed by the threat of electoral consequences.

It is just as predictable that the low PT elections should feature little evidence of this kind of influence. When turnout predictions are low and voters don't send compelling signals, we should expect candidates and presidents to feel more at liberty to set the agenda as they see fit. That is what happened in 1988 and 1996.

The Limits of the PT Scale

This is all well and good, but what happens to voter policy influence when elections are in the middle on the PT scale? This question prompted a careful reflection on the case histories in the middle compared to the high and the low categories. That, in turn, forced a realization that the opening proposition, while true, is incomplete. This is because there is more than one kind of policy influence. Voters sometimes do achieve a consensus and demand action on their own, as happened in 1960 and 1992. The remaining cases, however, show that there are other kinds of influence that do not depend in this straightforward way on the level of policy consensus and turnout.

For example, voters can also have a less direct impact on policy than that envisioned in our proposition; an influence that becomes manifest only when candidates or presidents choose or avoid problems or policies based on what they hope or fear voter reactions might be. Although the examples discussed here — 1988 and 1996 — do come from the bottom of the PT scale, and while a less unified electorate is indeed likely to be left with little else in the way of policy influence, low PT scores nevertheless are not a precondition for this indirect brand of influence. It can and does occur under all PT conditions.

Furthermore, some of the cases show that voters have been and might again be invited by candidates or presidents to endorse their policy proposals, potentially gaining a certain kind of influence when such endorsement proves to be critical to a president's chance for legislative success. As it happens, two of the three examples of this in the sample do fall in the PT midrange, but that is even more circumstantial, for the case stories make it clear that there is no necessary link whatever between the PT score and the emergence of such voter policy influence opportunities. Far more important than the PT score in these cases is presidential initiative, most notably a request for public endorsement. To sum up, we can count three different kinds of voter policy influence, but only one depends on the pre-existing levels of policy consensus and voter turnout.

From Numbers to Cases: The Typology

This realization necessarily shifted the focus from aggregate numbers to the contextual analysis of cases. The quantitative evidence shown in Table 1.1 and Table 1.2 allowed a preliminary sorting and comparing of elections for exploring the preliminary suppositions about the relationship among problem consensus, turnout, and influence. It also inspired deeper questions about the nature and variety of voter influence. We will have reason to refer back to the data in these tables throughout the book, including the remainder of this chapter. From this point forward, however, qualitative analysis of individual campaigns and elections and their policy consequences will show how voter influence actually works and why it varies.

The typology is summarized in Table 1.4. (Note that some of the entries may not be fully clear until one reads the relevant chapters.) The first type, *direct influence*, is the one predicted by the preliminary hypothesis. It is created by high-consensus voter demand that affects what new presidents put on the agenda. One can call these cases "voter driven." Here, both consensus and turnout do prefigure voter policy influence. As noted, such cases are rare. In the sample, only 1960 and 1992 qualify. Two other cases — 1968 and 1980 — also featured turnout and consensus figures above the 50 percent line. As later scrutiny of those cases will show, however, neither year's problem consensus featured demand characteristics consistent with direct voter influence. Only in 1960 and 1992 did turnout spike upward from previous levels, lending some urgency to what were clear, super-majority expectations for action on the Soviet threat and the budget deficit, respectively. Presidents Kennedy and Clinton, both first-termers eager for public approval, were highly sensitive to voter policy anxiety. Partly because of that, each took action: the Kennedy defense spending increases, and the Clinton deficit reduction budget. The voter influence, though limited, was proactive and direct, and it preceded the setting of policy. The details are in Chapter 2.

The second category is *anticipatory influence*. It emerges from the fact that most candidates and newly elected presidents do not face widespread voter policy anxiety, problem priorities supported by majorities, or even many special interest constituency demands that cannot be finessed or ignored. When voter demand is conflicted, fragmented, or otherwise politically manageable, candidates and presidents have the freedom to cut policy deals that voters are not a part of and often are not even made aware of unless and until any results become apparent. They can therefore only be judged by voters "after the fact." We call such deals "leader bargains." They are common occurrences, to be sure, but they are especially encouraged by low-turnout, low-consensus elections like those of 1988 and 1996, which

TABLE 1.4 Typology of Voter Influence on Policy

	Direct Influence	Legitimizing Influence	Anticipatory Influence
Origin	President responds to anxious voter demand	President wins public consent for policy	President bases policy choice on expected voter reaction
Frequency	2	1	7
Policy Stage	Pre-enactment	Pre-enactment	Contingent
Examples	1960 Cold war actions: increases in defense spending, nuclear capability, and foreign and military aid 1992 Deficit reduction	1980 Reagan tax and budget cuts	1989 Bailout of savings and loans 1990 Budget deal 1988 Bush–Dukakis de-emphasis of budget deficit 1996 Clinton–Dole implicit agreement to avoid entitlement debate

are featured in Chapter 3. In 1988, for example, candidates Bush and Dukakis both decided not to spend much time discussing the budget deficit, and also to avoid any discussion at all of the savings and loan crisis, because they both thought those were "no-win" campaign issues and they experienced little voter pressure to do otherwise. The only real chance for voter influence would come later, if and only if President Bush and Congress took anticipated voter reactions into account in enacting the savings and loan bailout of 1989 and the budget deal of 1990. Several mid-PT cases — 1956, 1968, 1972, 1976, and 1984 — also feature circumstances in which only the chance of anticipatory influence — deal makers choosing to take expected reactions into account — was available to voters, making this the largest of the influence categories. Because deal makers may or may not choose to take expected reactions into account, we have used the word "Contingent" on the "Policy Stage" row of Table 1.4. If deal makers do take expected reactions into account, the influence would occur in the pre-enactment stage. If they do not, there is no influence at any stage. In other words, whether or not there is influence, and at what stage (pre-enactment or no stage at all), is *contingent* on the subjective decisions of deal makers. These cases are discussed briefly in Chapter 3.

The last kind of voter influence is *legitimizing influence*. It becomes possible when candidates and new presidents want to claim voter support for their policies *before* they are enacted, in order to use the "consent of the governed" as leverage to get Congress to act. This is pre-enactment influence, but it is president driven, not voter driven. Most relevant are what are called the *claimed consent* cases. These are also relatively rare. Only three such cases appear in the sample, in 1964, 1980, and 2000 (see Chapter 4).

In 1964, Lyndon Johnson sold the country on the idea that he had won a mandate for education and civil rights (he hadn't). In 1980, Ronald Reagan seemed to have won an Election Day mandate for his tax and budget cuts (he hadn't either, and would be forced to run a postelection campaign to increase public support before he could get his program past a hostile Democratic House of Representatives). Many observers concluded (inaccurately) that both presidents had won mandates on Election Day because each had run on a few clear priorities and had achieved landslide victory margins aided by unpopular opponents.

In the third case, that of George W. Bush in 2000, losing the popular vote meant that he could make no claim of an Election Day mandate. Still, Bush took a page from Reagan's playbook and mounted an extensive postelection campaign for his own signature tax cut legislation. The public reaction to his campaign was ambivalent, but, by focusing on his tax-cut platform during campaign-style speaking visits to their states, Bush was able to convert enough Democratic legislators to his cause to ensure passage of his signature tax-cut bill.

Although all three candidates and presidents claimed the consent of the voters, only one of them — Ronald Reagan — actually had to demonstrate it. Voters were positioned to decide the fate of the Reagan proposal, so they exerted real legitimizing influence. This example, the only one of its kind in half a century, offers important guidance for the proposal described and illustrated in the final chapters.

Chapter 2
Direct Influence:
The Voter-Driven Cases

The most direct kind of voter policy influence becomes possible when a strong majority of the voting public agrees that a particular problem deserves the immediate attention of the national government. Such cases are called "voter driven" because the national agenda following any election that features such a consensus is largely fixed by popular demand. New presidents facing clear and widespread expectations have, in effect, been given their marching orders. Although they retain considerable freedom of choice concerning exactly how to proceed, such presidents do not have the political leeway to ignore or downplay the problems that trouble such a large proportion of the American people. They also have reason to test their plans in the court of public opinion before proceeding.

We have seen that within the sample of election cases used throughout this book, only 1960 and 1992 qualify as voter driven. As Table 1.1 showed, election turnout surged in those years, lending added urgency to what were clear, supermajority expectations that encouraged action on the Soviet threat and on the out-of-control federal budget deficit, respectively. As Table 1.3 showed, policy action related to the voters' top priorities followed these elections.

These cases deserve our attention because their histories show that voters got as close as possible, within the constraints of the U.S. political system, to the democratic ideal of voter-initiated, pre-enactment policy influence. That said, it must also be understood that maximum influence is, in the American system, still highly limited influence, as these cases also show. The structure of accountability built into the Constitution ensures it.

15

Consider the logic. Voter demand is obviously most threatening just before an election, when the costs to candidates of ignoring public preferences are the greatest, but the threat abruptly recedes once new presidents are installed; they are protected from voter reprisal by the fact that four years must elapse before they are held to account. This reality places limits on the postelection policy influence that high PT (problem consensus and turnout) and all other elections can create for voters. Other factors, the most important being the sensitivity of newly elected presidents to public opinion, must come into play if voters are to figure importantly in what happens once the election is over and the broad agenda has been set. If the two presidents featured in this chapter had not both been first-termers bent on reelection, for example, they would probably have been much less sensitive to public expectations as they faced their early challenges.

Insularity from public pressure was, of course, a deliberate design factor of the Constitution. It distinguishes the U.S. system from parliamentary systems where governments can fall at any time after a collapse of popular support amid passion and crisis, as shown, for example, by the change in Israeli prime ministers, from Barak to Sharon, in 2001. And it ensures that, in all essential respects, U.S. public policy will always be orchestrated by elected officials. That is the system that James Madison and his colleagues designed.

So the real question is, at any given time, how sensitive is that elite orchestration to the will of the American people? In 1960 and 1992, as we will see in this chapter, it was maximally sensitive.

1960: Meet the Soviet Threat

In 1960 the dominant national concern was the latent threat of war with the Soviet Union. Questions of peace and war were at the top of the policy agenda, together with widespread public anxiety over the cold war. This potentially deadly competition for world influence was sparked initially by Soviet expansionism after World War II; it progressively intensified with the emergence of a nuclear arms race, economic and technological competition, and increasingly confrontational Soviet–U.S. relations. Throughout the 1960 presidential campaign, these worsening relations led both the Democratic Party nominee, Massachusetts Senator John F. Kennedy, and the Republican Party nominee, Vice President Richard M. Nixon, to feature plans for improving America's strength and stature in the world. Other issues occasionally stirred passion and excitement on the campaign trail — Kennedy's glamour, controversy over his Catholicism, high-stakes TV debates, and a cliffhanger of a race — but these were not the things that did the most to shape important policy once the election was over. That distinction was reserved for the primary national problem: the Soviet threat.

Background

The major impetus for public anxiety in the run-up to the 1960 election was the Soviet Union's successful October 4, 1957, launching of *Sputnik*, the world's first orbiting satellite. This dramatic accomplishment created the impression that the Soviets had outpaced the United States in rocketry, thus shaking American public confidence in the superiority of American science and technology. The shock of the launching can be "compared only to that of Pearl Harbor." *Sputnik* frightened the American people because it implied that the Soviets had the capacity to project nuclear warheads to the American heartland (Greenstein 2000, 53). The flurry of defense- and education-related legislation passed in 1958 — presidential and congressional reaction to public panic at the launching of *Sputnik* (Pach and Richardson 1991, 178) — was one of the clearest examples of a voter-driven policy response in American history. Neither Democratic nor Republican officeholders wanted to face the voters in 1960 without being able to point to action taken to restore American technological primacy. Soviet Premier Nikita Khrushchev's bombastic visit to the United States in September 1959, best remembered for his using a shoe as a gavel during a United Nations address and for his boast that "we will bury you," added to the sense of foreboding. Democratic politicians began assailing the Eisenhower administration for failing to keep pace with the enemy. Charges of a "missile gap," heard originally in the mid-1950s, intensified after *Sputnik*. The missile gap was at the center of both the 1958 and 1960 election campaigns.

The irony is that there was no missile gap. President Eisenhower and Vice President Nixon both knew it, and they were also aware that the United States actually had a huge advantage over the Soviets in military missile development and in nuclear weaponry. In fact, the Soviets lagged badly in the production of usable warheads and intercontinental ballistic missiles (ICBMs), but the Eisenhower administration could not reveal this information without disclosing its U-2 reconnaissance plane spy program. That, Eisenhower feared, would worsen Soviet–American relations (which did happen when the Soviets finally shot down a U-2 spy plane in May 1960) and could push the Soviet leadership into a massive military buildup. With the "missile gap" charge left unanswered, critics began to speak of "a lack of national purpose" under Republican leadership (Patterson 1996, 418–22). Eisenhower would later be criticized for failing to refute the claim that there was a missile gap. His silence meant that Kennedy would enter the White House "pledged to bring about a major increase in the nation's missile capacity."

> Kennedy did just that, triggering an arms race between the Soviet Union and the United States that continued throughout the cold war. The upshot is a post-cold-war world burdened by stockpiles of

nuclear warheads that could destroy life on the planet many times over, an eventuality Eisenhower would have viewed with horror. (Greenstein 2000, 55)

The Campaign

The intensifying cold war and the public alarm it engendered represented a target of opportunity for the Democratic challenger. In the first debate with Nixon, Kennedy framed the issue: "The question before us all — the question that faces all Democrats and all Republicans — is, can freedom in the next generation conquer, or will the communists be successful — that's the great issue." He then went on the attack, hammering both the missile gap and the lack of national purpose, pledging to "get the country moving again." In the January 1960 speech announcing his candidacy, in the debates, and later in his inaugural address, Kennedy called for sacrifice: "The New Frontier is here whether we seek it or not — in uncharted areas of science and space, unsolved problems of peace and war" (quoted in Giglio 1991, 16). Nixon echoed Kennedy's identification of "the one great issue of the campaign: how to keep the peace without surrender of territory or principle, and how to preserve and extend freedom everywhere in the world" (Nixon 1962, 400).

Kennedy attacked Eisenhower for his failure to keep pace with the Soviet Union in education and technology, as well as ICBMs. He blamed the Eisenhower-Nixon administration for America's declining prestige in the world, especially among newly emerging nations in Africa and Asia, the key new "Third World" battleground of the cold war. He also pointed to the loss of Cuba to the Communists and the failure of the summit conference after the disastrous U-2 affair in May (Giglio 1991, 17). The U-2 crisis dashed hopes for détente and plunged the cold war back into freeze mode, where it remained through the campaign and well beyond the election.

Public Opinion

The American people were greatly disturbed by the Cold War and, as we have seen, were badly misinformed about the state of the arms race. A February 1960 Gallup Poll showed that a plurality — 47 to 33 percent — thought that the Soviet Union was ahead of the United States in development of missiles and rockets. The fear spawned by this competition was made apparent in a Gallup Poll published on June 3 showing that 71 percent of a national sample favored a law requiring each community in the United States to build public bomb shelters (Gallup 1972, 1671; see also Table 1.1). An earlier Gallup Poll, published on March 2, had reported that an "overwhelming majority" named issues dealing with foreign policy as "the most important problem facing the country today" (Gallup, 1972, 1656). Relatedly, a telephone survey of 1200 voters taken between August

TABLE 2.1 August 1960 Voter Issue Priorities

Keeping Ahead of the Russians
Developing Missiles
Keeping Prices Down
Civil Rights
Old Folks
Employment
States Rights
Farm Income

Source: Pool, Abelson and Popkin 1964, 86.

13 and 18 by a university research team yielded the rank ordering of the public's issue priorities depicted in Table 2.1. As is apparent, the first three priorities identified in the table deal with the emotional pushes and pulls of the effort to negotiate with a formidable adversary from a position of strength.

These poll results show that voters saw the Soviet challenge as the central issue facing the country in 1960. Although Kennedy played to their fears, he did so because he knew that Americans were already greatly concerned. His campaign rhetoric no doubt intensified public anxiety, but in no sense could he be accused of creating it. The people had already made it abundantly clear that the next president, whoever he turned out to be and whatever his margin of victory, would have as his first priority strengthening America's competitive position in the cold war.

Postelection Policy Action

Following a record turnout of nearly 63 percent, Kennedy was narrowly elected and began addressing the top priority. "Kennedy's proposed solution to the asserted and imaginary missile gap was simple," wrote biographer Geoffrey Perret, "spend more money. Lots more money. Security could only be found, Kennedy insisted, in more nuclear warheads, more long-range missiles" (2001, 268). As Table 1.3 showed, the new administration pushed for and got increases in defense spending, including provisions for enhanced nuclear capabilities, increases in foreign aid, and increases in military aid for U.S. allies. These funds supported an intensification of the arms and technology race, an increase in space exploration, and an increase in support for anticommunist movements around the globe.

The funding resulted from special requests Kennedy made to Congress in the early months of his presidency — January, April, and May, 1961 — as follow-ups to his campaign promises, but also prompted by worsening tension in the Soviet relationship. In an effort to signal his resolve to Soviet Premiere Khrushchev prior to their summit meeting in Vienna, Austria,

Kennedy appeared before Congress on May 25, 1961. Such an appearance was highly unusual so soon after a State of the Union Address, but, said Kennedy, "these are extraordinary times." Kennedy asked for an extra $2 billion for "new helicopters, new armored personnel carriers and new howitzers." The United States needed this equipment so it could respond to the threat of conventional warfare and Communist-inspired guerrilla conflicts (Perret 2001, 312). In his first six months in office, Kennedy asked for some $6 billion in new defense spending, increasing the defense budget to $47.5 billion, a figure that, at the time, constituted 52 percent of the federal budget. (By comparison, defense spending accounted for only about 16 percent of annual appropriations in the year 2000.)

In 1961 and 1962, a series of crises and confrontations further sharpened administration policy toward the Soviet Union. These included the Bay of Pigs invasion in April 1961, a threatened Communist takeover in Laos, an unsettling personal clash between Kennedy and Khrushchev at their June 1961 Vienna summit meeting, an ominous period of uncertainty when the Soviets erected the Berlin Wall in August, and the Cuban missile crisis in October 1962.

Evidence of Voter Influence

To what extent did Kennedy propose the policy measures that he did, and take the stands toward the Soviets that he took, because of the pressure of public expectations? Foreign policy crises absorbed most of Kennedy's attention during his short presidency. The fact that he was caught up in one crisis after another from the very beginning forced him to deal with the Soviet threat as the top priority, whatever the public thought and whether he wanted to or not. Public opinion was not the only source of influence on policy, but nevertheless Kennedy's sensitivity to public expectations was real and acute, especially in the first two years of his presidency. The various crises served only to heighten the already great importance he attached to sustaining broad support for his leadership.

It was no accident that Kennedy was the first president to incorporate the analysis of public opinion into the institutional functioning of the White House (Shapiro and Jacobs 2000, 15). From the beginning of his presidential candidacy until the end of his presidency, Kennedy sought to portray himself — and to convince the public to accept him — as second to none in his determination to meet the Soviet threat. By playing on public anxiety during his campaign, he deliberately intensified the expectations he knew he would have to meet if he won. He signaled his intent to meet those expectations in the promise stated in his inaugural address to "pay any price and bear any burden" to advance the cause of freedom in the world. This breathtaking pledge left him with little room to downsize expectations, but he was expressing the resolve he believed the people wanted. He expected to be held to strict account at every turn, but his razor-thin victory margin seemed to require both bold talk and evidence of his willingness to back up that talk with action.

Kennedy biographer Richard Reeves says "he often stuck a slip of paper into his pocket to remind himself of that tiny popular vote margin: 118,574 votes" (1993, 18). This suggests that his tenuous electoral standing was continually on his mind, a point also noted by others (e.g., Conley 2001, 147). Kennedy's constant preoccupation with his standing was consistent with the way he saw the cold war with the Soviets as an intense daily competition for the hearts and minds of a world as well as a national audience — in short, a war for public opinion. Kennedy's choice of words shows that he perceived and defined his presidential mission largely in terms of public reputation and prestige:

> I want to be *known* as the President at the end of four years, as one who not only held back the Communist tide but who also advanced the cause of freedom and rebuilt American *prestige*. (quoted in Reeves 1993, 54; italics mine)

Kennedy was acutely sensitive to the political and public-relations dimensions of every step he took. For example, in response to polls taken early in his administration, he played up his support for the Peace Corps, for better relations with allies, and for strengthening the United Nations, and he addressed the U.S. balance-of-payments problem (Jacobs and Shapiro 1962). As this suggests, Kennedy knew exactly what the people thought and expected, and he often took guidance from them in hopes of increasing their support.

A particularly revealing example of Kennedy's preoccupation with public opinion involved his reaction to a Gallup Poll showing 63 percent public disapproval of the civil rights Freedom Rides in the South. This high level of disapproval encouraged him to view such civil rights flare-ups as diversions from his real agenda — managing the cold war — and as a source of negative publicity that only helped the Communists. Especially in the early days, Kennedy saw everything from civil rights to the space race almost exclusively in terms of how it helped or hurt the U.S. position in the dangerous chess game with the Soviets.

Kennedy Television

Kennedy managed to create what may have been the most direct, personal, and emotionally charged relationship with the American people ever established by an American president. One important reason for this was the immediacy and the intimacy of television, used more frequently by Kennedy than any predecessor, and used more effectively by him than most subsequent presidents. Another reason was the atmosphere of unrelieved tension in the Soviet relationship, which Kennedy communicated to the American people through a series of somber television addresses, often alarming crisis pronouncements.

The early television addresses were sobering because they amounted to calls to prepare for sacrifice and for the possibility of war. These tense messages brought to life the immediacy of the dangers that forced Kennedy to call for national unity and resolve. The inaugural address set the tone. It featured Kennedy's commitment of the nation to do whatever was necessary to advance the cause of freedom, and it demanded that each American "ask not what your country can do for you, ask what you can do for your country."

The first foreign policy crisis involved a threatened Communist takeover in Laos, and Kennedy went on television within weeks of his inauguration to inform the public of his intent to resist and to ask for their support. Later, when the cost of resistance appeared too high, he went on TV again, on March 23, 1961, and in a compelling presentation asked the people to support his new policy of neutrality (Perret 2001, 303). By July, after the tension with the Soviets had increased to the point that Kennedy felt the need to signal anew his own resolve and to focus the public on the severity of the threat, he took to the airwaves again, on July 25. Part of the address simply announced his intention to expand the available instruments of war, including calls for new and larger stocks of conventional arms and ammunition, and for returning obsolete warships and B-47 strategic bombers to service, but most sobering to the public were the announcements that draft calls would be more than doubled and that Kennedy would ask Congress for more than $200 million to initiate a nuclear shelter program.

> "In the coming months," he declared solemnly, "I hope to let every citizen know what steps he can take without delay to protect his family in case of attack." It was a hair-raising experience for millions of Americans; war seemed frighteningly close that summer's night. (Perret 2001, 321)

Kennedy's preoccupation with sustaining unity and support is illustrated by an August 3 TV address asking the people to approve a tough line against the Soviets in Berlin. He was heartened when a later Gallup Poll indicated that 85 percent of Americans were willing to risk war to keep U.S. troops in Berlin.

The Cuban missile crisis was the occasion for the ultimate cold war television address describing the confrontation with the Soviets that brought the world to the brink of nuclear war. The high stakes meant that the outcome — a Soviet agreement to remove its missiles from Cuban soil — would be decisive for Kennedy's credibility as a leader. It would win for him the kind of respectful media treatment reserved for those presidents who successfully weather great crises (Liebovich 2001, 27–29).

Interspersed among these cold war pronouncements were frequent displays of Kennedy's most important public relations innovation: the live television press conference. He held sixty-three such sessions in his thirty-four months in the White House. Despite the "press conference" label, their primary purpose was less to inform and impress the media than to connect with the public. Kennedy wanted the American people to see and hear his answers and opening statements as he gave them, without their having to rely on newspaper accounts and headlines. The aim was to communicate with voters in a way that no newspaper could alter by interpretation or omission. "We couldn't survive without TV," remarked Kennedy to speechwriter Theodore Sorensen as they watched a rebroadcast of one of his press conferences (quoted in Sorensen 1965, 325).

Kennedy's unprecedented use of this forum let him display more of his talents than could be featured in formal television addresses about cold war dangers. The press conferences were showcases; lively and entertaining demonstrations of the Kennedy wit, charm, and polish as well as of his impressive command of the details of government operations. The exchanges with reporters seemed highly spontaneous. Each press conference was in fact a carefully rehearsed performance, however, aimed at projecting Kennedy's mastery of whatever difficulties confronted him at the moment.

The print press was indignant at Kennedy's use of live television. Journalists resented what they knew was an effort to reduce their role in mediating the communication between the president and the people. Kennedy, relaxed and informal, made highly effective use of his wit and self-deprecating humor to deflect and defuse the often loaded and critical questions of reporters. Told, for example, of a Republican resolution that he was a failure, he smiled and said "I am sure it was passed unanimously." When reporters complained that press conferences turned them into props for the president and the television industry, he replied, with a hint of sarcasm, that "it is highly beneficial [to news organizations] to have some twenty million Americans regularly...observe the incisive, the intelligent and the courteous qualities displayed by...Washington correspondents" (quoted in Sorensen 1965, 323).

The press might have been wary, but the public responded with delight to the spectacle of the president jousting with reporters and addressing his national audience casually and directly on live television. For the audience, the effect was reassuring as well as entertaining. The sessions featured welcome lighter moments of respite from the often grim news conveyed during speeches. They also offered clear evidence of presidential competence. Perhaps most important, the yin and yang of televised cold war speeches, interspersed with lively and humanizing press conferences, seemed to strengthen the bond between the young president and his national audience. That was of vital importance to Kennedy because it helped him to put across the idea that he was in fact doing what the American people had elected him to do. As biographer Geoffrey Perret concludes, Kennedy's press conferences were a public-relations triumph as great as President Franklin Roosevelt's fireside chats, helping to push his approval ratings to 80 percent. "The narrowness of his election made him weak on Capitol Hill, but popularity like this freed him to be strong in the world" (2001, 299).

Conclusion

It is clear, then, that Kennedy kept a watchful eye on public opinion and struggled both to shape and to respond to expectations. He did so for two main reasons. First, he believed that he needed to keep the public on board as a signal to the world that he was carrying out the will of the American people, which meant that he could face the Soviet challenge from a position of domestic strength. And second, he felt that his narrow margin of victory left him "on probation" with the public, which made it essential that he show broad support for every risky and potentially fateful foreign policy action that he took. He took comfort in the consistently high public affirmation of his presidential performance, but his self-confidence did not include the conviction that he was politically invulnerable. He understood that his political fortunes could change overnight — that unanticipated events could suddenly undermine his popularity and make him vulnerable to defeat in 1964 (Dallek, 2003). Every Kennedy biography makes it abundantly clear that reelection in 1964 was a driving force in his thinking. He worried, for example, that sluggish economic growth might outweigh foreign policy success on Election Day, and he resolved to lower unemployment and promote economic growth as his surest route to reelection (Perret, 2001, 295). Reelection was important not just as an end in itself, but also as validation of his mastery of the Soviet problem, which he knew to be the ultimate test of his presidency. That is why convincing the public that he was meeting that challenge was Kennedy's preoccupation from his first day as president to his last.

1992: Fix the Economy

Table 1.1 identified the public's top concern just before the 1992 election as a collection of threats not to international peace but to domestic prosperity. The Gallup organization summarized the national responses to its query about "the most important problem facing this country today" as "Economy/Jobs/Deficit." Fully 81 percent saw one or another of these problems as urgent. The message to all candidates for federal office was unmistakable: the voters expected the winners to fix the economy. As it happened, the economic indicators were already on the upswing as Election Day approached, but the good news had yet to reach the people.

Economic Anxiety

The slow recognition of an improving economy — seven weeks after Election Day 1992, economists announced that the recession had ended in

March 1991 — was one reason why the voters' anxiety about the economy set the tone of the presidential campaign (Ceaser and Busch 1993, 35). The man who lost the election, incumbent president George H.W. Bush, blamed the media for not spreading the word:

> When near the end of my term I said the economy was recovering the [media] stated, all but unanimously, that I was out of touch. The economy had indeed recovered. We handed Pres. Clinton a fast growing economy but none of the fall reporting that I recall credited us with any of this recovery. Just the opposite. (Bush 1998)

The people simply did not believe there was a recovery. In the fall of 1991, Bush's own internal polling found 80 percent of the public still agreed that "the country is in a recession right now" (Clymer 1993, A12). By November 1991, the public had grown even more pessimistic. A *Wall Street Journal/NBC News* poll showed that "32 percent of voters think the economy will get worse in the next year, while only 26 percent think it will get better," an almost exact reversal of the "better-worse" percentages from the previous month (Murray 1991, A1).

Unhappiness with the incumbent's unwillingness to address economic anxiety made an economic-policy debate all but certain during the 1992 campaign. The debate was shaped by the emergence of nontraditional candidates, most notably former Massachusetts senator Paul Tsongas and Texas billionaire H. Ross Perot. Neither Tsongas, a Democrat, nor Perot, an independent, had a real chance to win, but each helped to intensify the influence of mass economic anxiety on the campaigns of the eventual major party nominees.

Tsongas set the tone for the campaign year with his determination to be a "Johnny-one-note" on the economy. His message was that there could be no true economic revival without a strong manufacturing base. He backed it up with publication and promotion of an eighty-six-page issue booklet titled *A Call to Economic Arms* detailing his plans for economic reform. Perot and other candidates, including Arkansas Governor Bill Clinton and President George Bush, would all eventually produce their own booklet-length policy plans, making 1992 the "year of the booklet" in presidential politics (Feinsilber 1992, A14).

Tsongas managed to parlay his no-nonsense economic message into an upset victory over Bill Clinton in the Democratic primary in New Hampshire, where economic conditions were among the worst in the nation. More than anything else, the Tsongas New Hampshire victory established the perception — shared from then on by the national media and all other presidential candidates — that the voters were mobilized to demand a serious campaign focused on how best to fix the economy.

Ross Perot did more than anyone else to reinforce that message. He did so with an historically important "outsider" campaign that further intensified the public's demand for deficit reduction and economic growth. Perot acted to mobilize voters in several specific ways (detailed in Buchanan 1995). From his initial (February 20, 1992) appearance on *Larry King Live*, to his explosive ascent to the top spot in the polls in June (the only outsider candidate ever to achieve first place), to his quixotic departure from the race on July 17, to his reentry on October 1, Perot drew national public attention to the campaign as did no other person or event; he did this with winning debate performances, infomercials, and pronouncements stressing the budget deficit and the inadequacies of traditional politics and parties. He further entrenched the economic-policy focus initiated by Tsongas, and he forced the other candidates to address the federal budget deficit much more frequently and specifically than they would otherwise have done. Both individually and together with Tsongas, Perot was instrumental in generating the most substantive presidential campaign since the Reagan campaign of 1980, and in attracting the largest voter turnout since the 1960 presidential campaign — nearly 56 percent.

Ultimately, however, it was voter demand — sparked by economic anxiety and focused on by Tsongas and Perot — that forced a more substantive and participative campaign in 1992. By their response to pollsters, their primary votes, and their reactions to highly unusual outsider candidates, voters made it clear to the major party nominees that a different approach was needed. As *New York Times* reporter Robin Toner put it at campaign's end, "This was a big, sweeping, utterly serious campaign that left little in its path unchanged. ...From the New Hampshire primary on, the voters provided a merciless reality check on the candidates; those who strayed from the economy for very long were quickly punished" (1992: A1).

Voter Policy Influence

Voter anxiety clearly affected the tenor of the campaign. But what of voter influence on the major postelection policy action in Table1.3: the deficit reduction budget of 1993? Did the newly elected president, Bill Clinton, decide to make deficit reduction the centerpiece of his first budget proposal because of public alarm over the deficit and the perceived economic slowdown?

The answer is a qualified "yes." Voter sentiment, though not the only reason, was a big reason for Clinton's decision. Polls both before and after the election consistently put the public on the side of deficit reduction. Clinton was well aware of the impact that Ross Perot had had on the public's view of the deficit's urgency during the campaign. All of the candidates had been forced to respond by promising to reduce the deficit. Perot's own stringent deficit reduction plan "thrust the issue at Bush and Clinton," making it a question that "both would have to grapple with as long as Mr. Perot remain[ed] a factor in the Presidential equation" (Holmes 1992, A1). That view would be much repeated in the press. "With his strong emphasis on the need to reduce the federal deficit," wrote two *Wall Street Journal* reporters, "Mr. Perot may well increase the pressure on the other two candidates to address the issue in a more specific way" (Shribman and Noah 1992, A1).

For his part, Clinton had promised to cut the deficit in half by 1996; as Perot's influence increased, Clinton began to mention the deficit at least in passing in every speech. But neither he nor the people closest to him during the campaign yet believed that the deficit should be allowed to crowd out his "putting people first" agenda aimed at creating new opportunities for middle-class voters. At the October 15 presidential candidate debate, for example, he signaled his resistance to making the deficit his top priority. He clearly preferred that the early centerpiece of his economic strategy be increased "investment" spending for a job-creation program, with the deficit relegated to a subordinate place on his list of priorities.

The Clinton Conversion

Once Clinton was elected, his resistance to putting the deficit first prompted a major lobbying effort by a group of highly influential public figures. Federal Reserve Board chairman Alan Greenspan; several soon-to-be members of the new Clinton administration, such as Treasury Secretary Lloyd Bentsen, Office of Management and Budget Director Leon Panetta, and economic advisor Robert Rubin; plus such Democratic fiscal conservatives as Nebraska Senator Bob Kerry, among many others, began pressing the president-elect to embrace deficit reduction as the essential first step in the effort to jump-start the economy. Reducing the deficit, they argued, would free up investment capital for economic growth and would calm the fears of bondholders. That was necessary so that the latter wouldn't sell their bonds in alarm and drive interest rates up, further reducing the availability of investment capital. Instead, long-term bond rates would decline, further stimulating new capital investment. Later, when new projections showed the deficit problem to be larger than expected (Woodward 1994, 77), new deficit hawks were summoned to make similar arguments. Economists like Princeton University's Alan Blinder, for example, said lowering the deficit would help the national economy by freeing up savings for real investment rather than unproductive government bonds (Woodward 1994, 83). Also, a credible deficit reduction plan would convince bondholders to buy and sell at lower rates, thus making more investment capital available due to the decreased cost of borrowing.

In the face of this onslaught, Clinton gradually came to see the deficit fix as a better way to repair the economy than some of his campaign proposals. Perot's deficit-reduction message had clearly taken root all over the country. Clinton had started to come around, but it would not be until months after the inauguration that the message fully penetrated and unified the entire Clinton team, many of whom still considered it to be an alien Republican position.

Still, Clinton's public statements on the economy had begun to change, and reporters took the cue:

> [H]is rhetoric on the deficit has changed noticeably since the election. In the Oct. 15 debate, candidate Clinton declared: "I don't think a president should be judged solely on the deficit." But at a news conference last week [he] said: "The goal should be to restore economic growth, create jobs, raise incomes, *but you have to do it with a multiyear deficit-reduction plan...*". (Wessel and Birnbaum 1992, A1; italics mine)

Public opinion weighed in again. Clinton, who had just begun signaling his conversion to the deficit-reduction doctrine, was hit with a new *Wall Street Journal/NBC News* poll showing that 58 percent of respondents didn't believe him. Specifically, they doubted that he would achieve his stated campaign goal of halving the deficit by 1996. In his first newspaper interview after the election, he reaffirmed his commitment: "Bill Clinton, determined to convince the public and financial markets that he's serious about deficit reduction...repeatedly stressed his growing concern about the long term economic effects of the deficit" (Birnbaum and Frisby, 1992: A1).

The Internal Debate

Once installed in office, the Clinton team needed to go beyond rhetoric and formulate a concrete economic plan to be incorporated in their first budget submission to Congress. At this point, it became clear that his political consultants, those who had helped Clinton to craft the message that got him elected and who would be needed to help mount the effort to push the economic plan through Congress, were strongly resistant to the new deficit emphasis. Strategists James Carville and Paul Begala, pollster Stanley Greenberg, and media adviser Mandy Grunwald were among those who argued strenuously against abandoning the programs on which they had campaigned. Those who had helped elect Clinton smarted from the fact that almost every plank of the original Clinton agenda, the agenda that had propelled them to the White House, had been abandoned. Investments in such things as worker retraining had been scuttled; health-care reform was on hold; Oklahoma Senator David Boren, a New Democrat, was leading a movement for more deficit reduction via entitlement cuts; the middle-class tax cut had been abandoned, the populist themes downplayed; the stimulus package had been strangled; economic growth was foundering at less than 2 percent; and entitlement spending was still climbing. Worse, the consultants believed that making deficit reduction a priority would help the rich more than the middle class, the group that Bill Clinton had sought the presidency in order to help. Was Clinton forgetting why he had been elected president? "George Bush had just lost the presidency because he had broken his 'no new taxes' pledge," recalled Mandy Grunwald. "[A]nd there we were, breaking our promise to have a middle-class tax cut — and not doing nearly as much 'investment' as he had promised either" (quoted in Klein 2002, 52).

Years later, many of the Clinton administration's central characters would tell journalist Joe Klein that fellow journalist Bob Woodward's 1994 book, *The Agenda*, while accurate in its details, "underestimated the resolute quality of the [deficit reduction] operation." Klein quotes Hillary Clinton as saying that her husband "knew from the start that deficit reduction was the predicate, that we couldn't have a credible activist government unless we could get the budget under control" (2002, 48–49). Perhaps. But Clinton, a famously undisciplined and disorganized decision maker, seemed genuinely torn at the time, despite the prodeficit signals he was sending. And resolute or not, the fact is that Clinton could not bring himself to an early decision about budget specifics, priorities, or strategies. Discussion and debate thus continued for months, both inside the administration and in Congress, on the specifics of the economic plan. Clinton continued to be beset by deficit hawks on the one side and political advisors on the other, each pressing a different agenda in what was portrayed as a "fight for the President's soul" (Woodward, 1994).

When it became apparent that the deficit hawks in and outside the administration were winning the argument, the consultants hoped that the voters would help them to make the counterargument. They sought poll and focus-group evidence to show that the people did not want Clinton to abandon his investment plans in favor of deficit reduction. For the most part, they would be disappointed.

The Clinton public-opinion-monitoring effort was headed by Stanley Greenberg, who regularly sought to understand how the public was responding to the postelection effort to hammer out an economic policy. A Greenberg focus group conducted on December 6, 1992, showed no passion for the Clinton campaign agenda but instead a willingness to sacrifice to fix the economy if all interested parties were asked to contribute more or less equally to the recovery effort. This early postelection reading signaled that the people remained open to strong economic-recovery medicine such as deficit reduction.

When Clinton's effort to pass an economic stimulus package, a small portion of his campaign agenda, was defeated in an April 1993 Senate vote, it set off a sharp decline in his public-approval ratings. Greenberg's research showed that many people were under the impression that Clinton's entire economic plan had been defeated or was heading for defeat. Greenberg concluded that, to the American people, the death of the stimulus bill meant that gridlock still reigned supreme, and Clinton had not been able to overcome it (Woodward 1994, 173). This helped convince Clinton that simply getting something — almost anything — passed was just as important as what passed. By June 8, 1993, Greenberg's polls showed that 70 percent of the public rated Clinton's performance as only fair or poor (Woodward 1994, 226). Meanwhile, the message from Democrats in Congress was that the people in their states and districts were still clamoring for deficit reduction (Woodward 1994, 229). Near the end of June, Greenberg's polls were showing that economic growth and investments and deficit reduction were equally popular, but that the deficit-reduction message was "much cleaner and easier." The same polls suggested that it shouldn't be presented as an end in itself. Deficit reduction had to be seen as part of "putting our house in order," cleaning up the economy (Woodward 1994, 241).

At a July 3 meeting, Greenberg revealed new focus-group findings that showed that Clinton had still not educated the public about his economic priorities. People knew nothing about the Clinton economic plan except that it contained taxes. They didn't know the taxes fell on the rich, and they didn't know about the focus on deficit reduction (Woodward 1994, 246). The public, in short, was confused about the purpose of the Clinton economic plan. Internal White House debates had prevented Clinton from communicating a clear, specific message about what he was trying to accomplish. In Vice President Al Gore's words, Clinton was simply "too shaky and tentative" in both his public and his private pronouncements about the program (quoted in Woodward 1994: 280).

Later in July, Greenberg mounted yet another effort to grasp how people viewed the Clinton presidency and why they weren't connecting with him or his economic plan. Focus groups and polls showed again, as they had as far back as December 1992, that people most wanted not this or that specific economic plan, but an end to gridlock between the president and Congress (Woodward 1994, 269). Finally, on July 29, the House and Senate negotiators agreed on the tax provision of the Clinton plan: a modest 4.3-cent-a-gallon gasoline levy. On August 3, Clinton went on television to explain his plan, garnering a 48 to 41 percent favorable response in Greenberg's poll (Woodward 1994, 285). Shortly thereafter, the House passed the budget 218 to 216. The Senate was split down the middle, 50–50, with Vice President Gore breaking the tie in the administration's favor on August 6, 1993. After a heroic last-minute effort, and with no Republican votes in Congress, the Clinton forces had managed a narrow victory. The administration deficit hawks — aided by the New Democrats in the Senate, by a striking lack of support in Congress for the "putting people first" campaign agenda, and by a public that supported deficit reduction and demanded action throughout — had prevailed. The result was a five-year $500 billion deficit reduction budget.

Conclusion

There is more to the story than can be told here, but enough has been said to bring the lineaments of public influence clearly into focus. Clinton had begun his presidential campaign with the idea that the deficit did not need to be the top priority, and he concluded it by acknowledging its primacy. Public opinion had played a part in bringing about that change. Voters, with an assist from Perot, forced candidate Clinton to do something he would rather not have done: pay serious attention to the deficit. Later, public skepticism about continued gridlock had helped an elite group of deficit hawks to pressure President-Elect Clinton into giving the deficit priority over his other economic policy plans. Finally, after continued evidence of public support for deficit reduction and congressional action convinced the Clinton team to pull together, they managed to eke out a legislative victory that ratified their deficit reduction budget.

Voter-Driven Cases: Common Elements

What made public expectations influential in the early stages of the Kennedy and Clinton presidencies while policy was taking shape? Four factors stand out. The first is clarity. In these high PT cases, there is no doubt that each new president was expected to give priority attention to a specific problem. During the cold war, managing and dominating the relationship with the Soviet Union was the threshold test that voters used to judge Kennedy. For Clinton, the test was working with Congress to devise a plan to address the sluggish economy.

The second factor is majority support for the expectations. Table 1.1 showed that majority expectations are atypical. Widespread agreement on the most important problem has crystallized prior to only four of the last twelve elections. True, as Table 1.1 showed, the pre-election majorities in 1960 and 1992 were for very broad conceptions of the top-priority problems. In 1960, it was essentially "the Soviet Union is the problem." In 1992, it was "Economy/Jobs/Deficit." Public calls for more specific action, such as deficit reduction in 1992 and 1993, registered less-than-majority support when the poll responses for those years are disaggregated; the weight of majority anxiety surrounding the broader problem, however, added greater urgency and momentum to the eventual call for specific action than would have been the case without that added boost. For example, even thought the deficit was the top issue in 1988 (see Table 1.1), no election-inspired momentum behind deficit reduction existed in 1989 because there was no majority insistence on some kind of action behind it.

The third factor is stability; that is, the expectations endured across time. This is another comparative rarity for public opinion, which is typically more fluid and transitory. By 1960 and 1992, public anxiety about the top problems had been building for years.

Last, the circumstances of particular presidents matter greatly. Kennedy and Clinton were both first-termers who planned to run again, and as a result they were both keenly attuned to public expectations. Incumbents with reelection hopes are always the most prone to respond to clear and credible public expectations.

Out-Of-Season Voter Influence

Before turning to other kinds of voter influence, it is worth noting that not all direct public influence on policy making unfolds in the immediate aftermath of a presidential election. Such influence can also occur at some remove from an actual election season, as politicians monitor public opinion with the next election in mind. The effect of this influence is most likely when unexpected events or circumstances provoke a strong public reaction that elected officials see as requiring a timely policy response.

One example has already been given: the legislative response to public panic in the aftermath of the *Sputnik* launch. Another example was the 1997 budget agreement between President Clinton and the Republican Congress, triggered by the widespread perception in Washington that the public had blamed the Republicans in Congress for the government shutdowns of 1995 and 1996 and had punished the Republicans at the polls in 1996. The message received by both sides was that they had better find a way to settle the latest dispute over spending priorities. The result was the agreement to balance the budget by the year 2002. Intense partisans who saw any agreement with the opposition as ideological treason pressed to keep fighting, but the leaders on both sides decided not only to deal but to label the result a "bipartisan" agreement. They did so because they had learned to regard poll evidence of public displeasure with the state of budget politics as too dangerous to ignore. The threat of electoral reprisal had become entirely credible (Buchanan 2004).

Conclusion

What unites all of these cases and creates responsive politicians are clear voter expectations backed by the promise of support or the threat of reprisal; if high PT elections have the best chance to cue this sort of responsiveness, however, Table 1.1 tells us not to expect many such cues. In fact, most candidates and newly elected presidents do not face widespread policy anxiety that is linked to specific policy demands. This creates the "wiggle room" that enables them to cut policy deals that voters aren't part of and that they can judge only after the fact. Such deals are called "leader bargains," and they are the subject of the next chapter.

Chapter 3
Anticipatory Influence:
The Leader-Bargain Cases

All legislation and most other forms of policy action involve bargaining among presidents, members of Congress, and other elites. In other words, leader bargains happen all the time (Dahl 1998, 113). What varies are the nature and the extent of public influence on the evolution of any particular policy bargain at each important stage: problem definition, review of solution options, and choice of policy action.

The extent of public influence before policy has been enacted depends on the state of voter demand concerning the subject of the bargain and the proximity of the next election. So far as influence is concerned, there is no better time than the run-up to a presidential election for the American people to signal their policy preferences, but there is no assurance that they will do so in an effective way, that is, by signaling a strong, intensely felt consensus that candidates would be ill advised to ignore. The fact is that policy consensus in the electorate is often smaller than a majority, with concern scattered across many issues that attract only single-digit poll support. Turnout is also often low. Given such evidence of voter disagreement on priorities and of indifference to a particular election, candidates are more at liberty to set campaign agendas designed to serve their own electoral interests. If elected in such circumstances, candidates are similarly freer to promote agendas of their own choosing.

All is not lost, however. Although voters are often shut out from helping to shape policy *choice*, they can still judge the *results* at the next election. And when candidates and presidents know that they may be held accountable for results at the next election, this may prompt some if not all such figures to anticipate voter reactions as they set policy and perhaps choose or avoid particular policies. In such situations, leaders are either inhibited or encouraged by their own expectations of possible future electoral reward or punishment. When this happens, voters may be said to exert *anticipatory influence* on the policy priorities and choices of those leaders who take voter wishes into account. Leader idiosyncrasies make this brand of influence contingent and uncertain, but it is influence nonetheless. In any event, lack of direct pre-enactment influence, coupled with a chance for anticipatory influence, describe the possibilities open to voters in the leader-bargain cases reviewed in this chapter.

This chapter will present several examples, but we start with an extended review of 1988 and 1996 because, as Table 1.2 showed, they are the lowest PT (problem consensus and turnout) elections in our sample of twelve. The contrast between these elections and the *voter-driven* cases of 1960 and 1992 could not be starker, and it begins with issues. Whereas truly big questions of peace and prosperity were of paramount concern in 1960 and 1992, the 1988 and 1996 campaigns were preoccupied with such lesser matters as pollution in Boston Harbor and V-chip technology — important to some people, to be sure, but not near the top of any reasonable conception of the priorities of the national agenda. As the following two case narratives will show, as a result of fragmented voter demand, candidates found it both possible and tempting to use issue evasion and opportunism during these campaigns, which left the choices on some of the biggest policy questions facing the country to both pre- and postelection leader bargains that featured minimal public input.

1988: The Year of the Handlers

No shortage of major national policy problems existed as the 1988 presidential election approached. One nonpartisan effort to distill a short list of the most important problems from think-tank and foundation reports identified the "big four" policy problems as the federal budget deficit, then-lagging U.S. international economic competitiveness, a clarification of U.S. foreign policy, and domestic poverty (Buchanan 1988). The problems were related to one another in a variety of ways, but the most compelling link was cost. Before anyone could increase spending to enhance competitiveness or alleviate poverty, the out-of-control deficit would have to be tamed. The deficit was also a drag on the economy, draining investment dollars away from industrial expansion into unproductive Treasury debt instruments.

Another problem, little noticed by think tanks or media before the election, and almost completely unknown to the public, would loom large for the next president. This was the savings and loan crisis, later described as the largest financial policy debacle in American history. Mainly as a result of the deregulatory fervor of the Reagan administration and of laws passed in the early 1980s, it became possible for savings and loan (S&L) institutions to invest their deposited funds recklessly, secure in the knowledge that their losses would be covered by the Federal Savings and Loan Insurance Corporation.

This state of affairs was largely a consequence of the ordinary operation of a generally accepted political process in which short-term political incentives routinely override concern for potential long-term costs. In this case, the culprits were S&L executives and other big campaign contributors who lobbied Congress for deregulation of the S&L industry; the members of Congress who voted to grant the request; and the president — Ronald Reagan — who signed the Garn–St. Germain Act in 1982.

The act allowed the S&Ls to expand their lending capacities beyond home mortgages, their traditional focus, into far riskier investment vehicles. It also increased the Federal Deposit Insurance limit from $40,000 to $100,000. Thus, when the S&Ls began to fail, the act had made the government a full 150 percent more responsible for the bailout of depositors (Greene 2000, 81). Although only a small percentage of the failure was attributable to outright fraud, huge losses would result (Rom 1996). Estimates of the cost of covering the resulting losses range from $200 to $500 billion (Shuman 1992, 202–209). Efforts to call attention to the ever-increasing drain on the federal treasury, made by prominent economists, government accountants, and a top government regulator, began as early as 1981, but not until after the 1988 election and the inauguration of a new president did the government move to close down insolvent S&L institutions.

Political Context

Not surprisingly, no candidate chose to sound the alarm during the 1988 campaign. In fact, none of the daunting problems awaiting the next president and Congress managed to generate much political momentum, let alone an atmosphere of crisis, during the campaign. As Robert Teeter, Republican candidate George H.W. Bush's pollster put it: "[There were] no big peace-and-prosperity issues out there"; only a widely felt unease about the unraveling social fabric of the country (quoted in Goldman and Mathews 1989, 362). The economic indicators were generally positive, which induced a measure of public indifference to the presidential race. Median family income had risen 10 percent since 1981. Seventeen million new jobs had been created during the Reagan-Bush administration. Inflation and interest rates were down. Majorities were telling pollsters that the country was "on the right track" economically (Drew 1989, 272–73). The S&L problem was nearing crisis proportions but was still essentially invisible. It would receive no media attention at all during the campaign because, as one journalist put it, "It was a numbers story, not a people story" (Hume 1990, A25). It was complicated, boring to most journalists, and did not lend itself to the kind of short, simple coverage needed for effective television. Not until housing developments were auctioned off, S&L officials indicted, and members of Congress investigated, were news organizations given the kinds of story lines they preferred (Fiorina and Peterson 1998, 287).

The most visible and troubling economic indicator during the campaign was the deficit. It received substantial attention from a number of newspapers, which not only explained the issue but also occasionally chastised the candidates for ducking it. The *Wall Street Journal*, for example, featured an issue series on what it termed "the absent agenda," highlighting the deficit and other neglected issues (Buchanan 1991, 59).

Voter Detachment

Ordinary citizens, however, who get most of their news from television, saw little mention of the deficit on the TV news and heard even less from the candidates. Nor was there direct experience of deficit-inspired pain in their daily lives to remind them of the problem. Newspaper attention to the deficit did help to elevate the issue to the top rank among public priorities by campaign's end (Table 1.1), but even though no other issue was identified by a higher percentage of prospective voters, its endorsement by just 23 percent was never a strong enough public signal to compel the candidates to emphasize it or any other policy issue. Two other issues — drugs and homelessness — also achieved low double-digit percentage support as the "most important presidential problems," followed by several others in the high single digits (Buchanan 1991, 90). There was, in short, no strong public consensus on the most important problem facing the next president.

Candidate Incentives

The lack of a strong public consensus meant that the candidates had little reason to talk up the deficit any more than they did the S&L problem. They knew that a deficit fix would require unpopular spending cuts or tax increases or both, and thus they wanted to avoid the issue as much as possible. In fact, the most memorable line of George Bush's acceptance speech at the Republican national convention was an unequivocal promise not to raise taxes: "The Congress will push me to raise taxes, and I'll say no, and they'll push, and I'll say no, and they'll push again. And all I can say to them is: read my lips. No new taxes" (quoted in Greene 2000, 37).

When it became clear that public pressure would not grow strong enough to force the candidates to address the deficit, Bush and his Democratic opponent, Massachusetts Governor Michael Dukakis, treated it like they treated the S&L problem — with studied neglect. Each had a rhetorical answer to the occasional reporter's query about his deficit plans. For Bush, it was the "flexible freeze" in federal spending; for Dukakis, a promise to raise taxes only as "a last resort," which he clearly hoped to avoid. But their neglect of the deficit did capture press attention. "Mum's the word on the deficit," ran one headline (Taylor 1988).

Other issues got more attention from the candidates. Dukakis made a concerted effort to run a substantive race, and by campaign's end he had managed to make several of his positions known to a majority of a national sample of voters. Most prominent among these were his call for universal health care and for "good jobs at good wages." Bush's stance in favor of capital punishment became even more widely known than his no-new-taxes pledge (Buchanan 2004). Stung by later criticism that their campaign had evaded the real issues, Bush operatives would claim that their candidate had advanced no fewer than 207 policy proposals (Goldman and Mathews 1989 355).

However many issues Bush advanced, his critics had it right. The Bush campaign was never really about issues; it was about figuring out how an underdog could come from behind to win. Bush campaign staff research showed convincingly that the only way to win was by going on the attack. Bush's own poll-proven negatives were high, and no positive issue or favorable Bush characteristic had enough impact when tested in focus groups or polls to counteract his drawbacks. They included an indistinct image and a sixteen-point disadvantage against Dukakis in a Gallup Poll taken May 13–16, 1988. Because two-term incumbent Ronald Reagan could not be reelected, the 1988 contest was necessarily about a change at the top. The goal in a no-incumbent race that was not constrained by a voter-inspired policy agenda was simple: Make Bush look like a better choice than Dukakis.

The way to make Bush look better became obvious in a famous series of Paramus, New Jersey, focus groups conducted in May 1988. The thirty blue- and white-collar Democrats who participated — all former Reagan supporters — were chosen because of that, and also because each initially planned to vote for Dukakis. When they were told of the Massachusetts governor's veto of a 1977 Pledge of Allegiance bill, however, and of the prison furlough program that released convicted murderer Willie Horton, an African American, half of the participants turned against Dukakis. Bush campaign manager Lee Atwater described his reaction as one of those "ah-hah!" moments. "I realized right there that we had the wherewithal to win...and that the sky was the limit on Dukakis's negatives (quoted in Taylor and Broder 1988, 14).

The only potential sticking point was Bush. A man described by some political opponents as a "wimp," and believed by his closest friends to prefer not just a "kinder and gentler" but also a nobler approach to politics, might have resisted an attack strategy. His handlers, however, managed to convince him that the other side had started it:

> Bush's game was horseshoes, not alley fighting; it was easier to get him down and dirty if you persuaded him that he had been wronged and that the only manly thing to do was fight back. When

he came home from his convention-week camping trip, Ailes, Atwater and Barbara Bush were waiting with the news that the Democrats had just spent four nights punching his lights out on prime-time TV, chorusing "Where was George?" and hooting that he had been born with a silver foot in his mouth. (Goldman and Mathews 1989, 356)

Thereafter, the Bush campaign relentlessly hammered the political weaknesses of Michael Dukakis. He was portrayed in advertising and on the stump as an idealistic liberal who was dangerously naïve about crime and criminals and who was out of touch with mainstream American values. The Bush camp converted the election into a "referendum on the failed policy of the governor of Massachusetts…rather than on the performance of the incumbent [Reagan-Bush] administration or the leadership or judgment of the G.O.P. nominee (Ornstein and Schmitt 1989, 44). The problems sure to confront the next president were ignored. It was, in the end, a carefully orchestrated, often misleading, and to many a thoroughly mean-spirited attack that drove policy to the sidelines and disgusted much of the public.

It was devastatingly effective, however. It could not have worked if voters did not have some misgivings of their own about Dukakis, but the audacity of the strategy played a part in its success with both media and voters. Prior to 1988, the "killer" potential of attack ads had been fully exploited only in state and local races. The Bush campaign was the first at the presidential level to make attacks the strategic centerpiece, the first at that level to employ coded racial appeals in their ads, and the first to so thoroughly downplay the real business of the presidency (Goldman and Mathews, 1989, 360). The Bush team also successfully challenged the then-conventional wisdom that voters will punish departures from strict truthfulness in one candidate's allegations against the other (Jamieson 1988).

The mainstream media were enthralled. Reporters with such new and provocative material to cover devoted most of their attention to the novelties and spent little time pressing the candidates to discuss the national policy agenda. Media coverage emphasized Bush's attacks; photo ops at flag factories; ads featuring Willie Horton, who had committed several crimes after being furloughed from prison; and horse-race polls that confirmed the effectiveness of the Bush strategy. It was not until mid October, as polls showed increasing public discomfort with the aggressive tone of the campaign, that news stories even began to take note of public disgust and inaccuracies in the candidate's advertising (Buchanan 1991, 69). Dukakis did not capitalize. He had every reason to respond in kind to the Bush onslaught, but he resisted pressure from his campaign aides to do so (Germond and Witcover 1989, 465). He clung doggedly to his issue agenda, and by the time he was persuaded to strike back it was too late.

Conclusion: Voters Trumped

With no effective political opposition or public backlash, Bush was able to dictate the content and tone of the campaign. This had two major consequences. The first was a victory for Bush that had looked impossible six months earlier. That vindicated his handlers in the eyes of political professionals: "Bush's campaign was a technical masterpiece — an example of brilliant exploitation of the new political technology (Taylor 1989, 7). Many outside the political world were appalled, however. Voter turnout sank to its lowest point in more than sixty years. In an election wrap-up, CBS News anchorman Dan Rather asked correspondent Ed Bradley if voter reaction was as negative as that of the press and pundits. "No question, Dan," Bradley replied. "Most people thought that both of the candidates spent more time attacking the other man than they did explaining their own position — but they blame George Bush more for that negative tone" (quoted in Cramer, 1992: 1021).

The second major consequence was for postelection policy. The two most pressing among the foreseeable problems — the federal budget deficit and the S&L crisis — would indeed be addressed by President Bush and the Congress, and in relatively short order: the latter by the Financial Institutions Reform, Recovery, and Enforcement Act of 1989 (which bailed out failed S&Ls with federal money, adding hundreds of billions to the deficit over a period of years), and the former by the Omnibus Budget Reconciliation Act of 1990 (which combined an income tax hike for the wealthiest Americans and cuts in entitlement and discretionary programs to produce $500 billion in deficit reduction over five years).

Both of these measures proved to be effective. The budget deal, though politically costly to President Bush and not a full cure, nonetheless helped to put the budget deficit on a solution trajectory. The cost to Bush — loss of the presidency in 1992 — is of particular interest because he had to pay for failing to meet the policy expectations of his core constituency. The conventional wisdom is that the public voted him out in 1992 not because he raised taxes in a deal with the Democrats but because he broke his word in order to do it (Deficit Politics Returns 2002, A22). Most likely it was both the tax increase and the breach of faith, because many in the right wing of the Republican Party were as enraged at the one as at the other. It is curious that a president who was initially quite willing to do what was politically expedient in order to get elected (i.e., to promise not to raise taxes knowing he would have to break the promise) would later abandon expediency in order to do what he thought was right (i.e., to accept tax increases knowing full well it could cost him the presidency). Bush's explanation does not shed much light on his change of heart. He told one interviewer that he "didn't really want to" abandon his pledge not to raise taxes, but felt that he had to in order to balance the budget (Greene 2000, 80). Whatever the reason, the anticipation of sure political punishment did not work as a deterrent to unpopular policy, at least for this president. This is a case in which voters inflicted punishment, but they did not wield policy influence.

The S&L drama was quite different because it unfolded almost entirely outside of public awareness. The bailout successfully resolved a costly and embarrassing national problem, but there was little opportunity for the public to notice because citizen attention had been deliberately evaded by leader bargains at both the problem-recognition and the policy-making stages. Whether greater media attention to the S&L problem during the campaign would have increased the salience of the issue to the public is uncertain, but the lack of campaign discussion or media scrutiny denied voters the opportunity to decide for themselves or to pass informed judgment on the bailout.

1996: Over before It Started

1996 "will almost certainly be remembered as one of the dullest Presidential campaigns in recent times…the boring election," concluded one high-profile newspaper summary (Nagourney 1996, S4, 1). The signs were plentiful. Voter turnout, up sharply four years earlier, fell in 1996 to scarcely 49 percent, the lowest level in 72 years. Candidate debates, usually the campaign spectacle that voters find most interesting, drew far smaller audiences than they had in 1992 (Bark 1996, 20A). A *New York Times* poll taken about two weeks before Election Day found just 44 percent willing to describe the campaign as "interesting," while 50 percent called it "dull" (Berke 1996, A1). A Princeton Survey Research Associates poll taken for the Markle Foundation's Presidential Election Watch showed that, by mid September, 66 percent had already decided which candidate to support, compared to only 49 percent at the same point in 1988 (Princeton Survey Research Associates 1997).

Why was the campaign so boring? Not because there was nothing of importance for candidates to discuss. As in 1988, many unresolved national problems clamored for attention, each of which implicated the interests of large numbers of Americans. For example, the federal budget deficit had not yet been eliminated. The consensus among journalists, academics, and candid politicians was that it was not too early to begin debating the options for addressing the Social Security and Medicare funding shortfalls sure to follow the retirement of the Baby Boom generation beginning in 2013 (Darman 1996, S4, 9). Other problems ripe for campaign debate included the U.S. role in the evolving post–cold war world, the access and affordability crises of a health-care system that still excluded some 40 million Americans who lacked health insurance, the problems created by the 1996 welfare reform legislation, campaign finance and other political reforms, and chronic partisan differences over the proper role of government. As journalist Adam Nagourney put it: "What the people might have approved this year — had Mr. Dole and Mr.Clinton been more obliging — was either of the competing views of government presented by House Republicans in 1994 or by the more governmentally ambitious Mr. Clinton who ran in 1992" (Nagourney 1996, S4, 1).

It was not to be, however. Paradoxically, a high-stakes policy argument between president and Congress had been settled in the months before the 1996 campaign got under way, leaving the public with little appetite for more political conflict. Voters were putting no pressure on the incumbent president and reelection candidate, Democrat Bill Clinton, or on the Republican nominee, former Kansas senator Bob Dole, to address any particular problem. That left the candidates scrambling to find issues that could move a lethargic electorate. The result, as former Bush budget director Richard Darman put it, was that "both candidates offer[ed] the voters attractive tax cuts — what Ross Perot has termed 'free candy just before elections'" (1996, S4, 9).

Table 1.1 showed that 1996 featured not only low turnout but also a submajority and low-intensity consensus — 34 percent — on the most important problem — a pastiche of economic concerns. What had become of the anxiety that drove voters to the polls in record numbers just four years earlier? For one thing, the economy had improved dramatically. For another, candidate Clinton had managed to frame and settle the real policy argument well before the campaign started, effectively clinching reelection. His method was to convince a winning coalition of voters to see the election as their only chance to scuttle an unpopular Republican policy agenda. In that sense, 1996 voters exercised a significant form of preventative policy influence. But as happened in 1988, for different reasons, they were given no real chance to weigh or endorse the priority agenda of the future.

Clinton Primes the Voters

The real fight for the presidency began with the Republican takeover of Congress in 1994 and ended early in 1996, when the people began making it clear to pollsters that they rejected much of the Republican agenda and favored Clinton as a check against Republican "extremism." In the interim, President Clinton and the Republican leadership in Congress waged a war over the policy differences implicit in their conflicting budget priorities. Clinton embraced the popular parts of the Republican agenda — including a commitment to balance the budget within seven years and a stringent version of welfare reform that alienated the liberal wing of the Democratic Party — but he rejected the parts he knew to be unpopular, including cuts in Medicare, Medicaid, education, and environmental protection.

A key part of his effort to solidify public support was an unusual television advertising campaign that began far earlier than usual — in July 1995

— in twenty key swing states (Goldman 1995, B8). Most of the ads were tailored to remind voters that Republicans sought to cut popular programs. One typical commercial ran in April 1996 in Lansing, Michigan; as it was later described, it stated that "Mr. Clinton wanted to 'preserve Medicare' and 'save anti-drug programs.' But Speaker Newt Gingrich and Bob Dole, the Senate Majority Leader and then the leading Republican candidate for President, were out to block him, the narrator warned. 'Dole-Gingrich vote no – no to American's families'" (Bennet, November 10, 1998: A1).

Then, in late 1995 and early 1996, Clinton vetoed a pair of Republican budgets that included the unpopular cuts. Republicans responded by refusing to pass continuing resolutions that would have enabled the government to continue operations until an agreement was reached. This resulted in two relatively brief government shutdowns, which intensified media coverage of the policy dispute. Clinton then began a series of speeches and radio addresses to further stigmatize the Republicans as outside the mainstream and to build his advantage in the polls (Ceaser and Busch 1997, 44).

The ads, speeches, and radio addresses clearly matched what many voters were already thinking. Together with the government shutdowns, they helped Clinton win the public-relations war and, eventually, the election. The proof was in a *New York Times* poll taken late in the campaign that showed that the public remained deeply suspicious of Republican plans for fixing Medicare, disapproving by 56 to 25 percent (Clymer 1996). Clinton strategist Dick Morris would later claim that the election was over a full year before Election Day (Morris 1997, 151). More credible sources reached similar conclusions. Said a postelection *New York Times* editorial: "Campaign historians will probably identify the day the Government shut down as the day Mr. Clinton began his political revival" (Campaign '96 R.I.P. 1996: S4, 14.) Said Clinton opponent Bob Dole: "History will show that, because of the ad campaign, the election — for all practical purposes — was decided by early 1996, long before Republicans had a nominee" (Dole 1998, A18).

The Traditional Campaign

With one big policy argument settled and the race for the White House seemingly over before it started, little was left to attract media or voter attention to the election. The best hope of reviving what had become an anticlimactic campaign rested with outsider candidates, but only if they could conjure up a new policy debate and inject enough uncertainty in the outcome to rekindle interest. Two prime prospects were on the stage: Ross Perot and Colin Powell.

Perot, who had a major impact on both the policy debate and voter turnout in 1992, managed to get his Reform Party slate on all 50 state ballots for another try in 1996. By then his star was in decline, however, and he was not the attraction he had been. An increasingly quirky reputation and a less promising 1996 issue debate meant less media coverage and a less attentive public. For example, when Perot debuted his first half-hour infomercial in October 1992, pitching the importance of the budget deficit and demanding strong corrective action, it was a surprise ratings success, tying for thirty-second place among ninety prime-time television programs, and seen in 11.2 million households. A Perot infomercial broadcast on September 1, 1996, however, ranked just 104th among the week's 107 prime-time programs and was seen in fewer than 2 million households, according to Nielson Media Research (Bark 1996, 6A). Perot's standing in the polls never approached his 1992 highs. Worse, his 1996 poll numbers declined from 18 percent in the early spring to single-digit levels near Election Day. The eccentric Texan might nevertheless have been able to stir greater public interest in himself and his issues had he not been thwarted by the networks' refusal to sell him additional broadcast time (Stahl, 1996, 6A), and had he not been barred by the Commission on Presidential Debates from doing again what had so boosted his campaign 1992: participate in the candidate debates. But thwarted he was, with the result that he had little impact on the campaign.

With Perot marginalized, the best chance for an upsurge of interest would have been a decision by retired general and former Joint Chiefs of Staff chair Colin Powell, then the latest nonpartisan outsider to capture America's fancy, to run for president. He had dominated the invisible primary season by touring the nation to promote his memoirs, striking fear in the hearts of potential competitors. Some believed that Powell, who did not even disclose his political affiliation (Republican) until the day he announced he would *not* run for president, could have been elected as an Independent (e.g., Greenfield 1995, A11). He chose not to run, however, and his withdrawal disappointed millions, sending public interest in the presidential campaign to new lows (Rosenthal 1995).

These developments freed candidates Clinton and Dole to search for themes that could attract the votes of whoever did show up at the polls. Clinton used focus groups to learn what prospective voters wanted, then gave it to them in the form of proposals that proved to be popular. Markle Foundation polling showed that the three most widely supported candidate issue positions in the week before the election were Clinton initiatives: a proposal to spend $2.75 billion to improve the reading skills of school children in grades K through 3, endorsed by 71 percent of the population; a proposed $3.4 billion package of tax breaks and other incentives to encourage businesses to create jobs for people leaving the welfare rolls, endorsed by 67 percent; and a "targeted tax cut" proposal aimed at poor working families and middle-class families with children, supported by 66 percent (Buchanan 2004, 90).

All of these proposals could be defended as worthy. All were enthusiastically received by large majorities of prospective voters. But they were not on a par, in the hierarchy of national importance, with the issues that had shut the government down, or with such looming presidential problems as how to fix Social Security and Medicare. Nor was Republican candidate Bob Dole's call for a 15 percent across-the-board tax cut, although it was the centerpiece of his campaign and was supported by a majority — 51 percent — in the Markle poll. The Dole proposal came under increasing fire as the campaign wore on. One prospective voter interviewed in an October *Wall Street Journal* survey summarized the consensus when he described it as "too blatant a pander," given Dole's long record of opposition to just such tax cuts, and bad policy to boot, given the still-sizable budget deficit (Shafer 1996, A1).

With a lackluster policy debate and neither Colin Powell nor Ross Perot as attractions, the news media reduced their coverage of the campaign dramatically. Coding research showed that the major television networks — ABC, CBS, and NBC — offered 54 percent less election coverage in 1996 than in 1992. The same study showed that the coverage emphasized the candidates' conflicts over issues, and that the candidates' actual speeches and ads were much more positive in tone than they were portrayed in news accounts (Executive Summary 1998, 5). Needless to say, reduced coverage that stoked political cynicism did little to increase interest in the campaign or to encourage voting.

Conclusion: Let Us Share the Blame

In what campaign strategists in both camps saw as the last and best chance to alter the dynamic of the campaign before a live audience of millions, the candidates squared off in early October in the first of two nationally televised debates. In the sharpest exchange on a major issue in that debate, Dole attacked Clinton for his long-standing and highly effective assault on Republican plans to curb the growth of Medicare spending. "Stop scaring the seniors, Mr. President," he said. He then called for a truce on the Medicare issue, saying it should be taken up by a commission. Clinton immediately supported the proposal (Berke 1996, A1). Little more was said about Medicare by either candidate for the balance of the campaign. The Clinton-Dole debate exchange over Medicare was noteworthy because it may have been the only time in presidential-campaign history that the two major party nominees for president struck a bargain *in public,* before an audience of millions, to take a major national issue off the table and relegate it to a forum that both knew would be designed to ensure bipartisan blame sharing.

The commission agreement would be floated early in the second Clinton administration, but it never got off the ground. Clinton did convene a White House conference on Social Security reform in 1998, and he called for bipartisan action again in his State of the Union address in 1999, but he left office without resolving the issue, despite the opportunity represented by the unexpected emergence of budget surpluses (Brode 1999, A17). Why did it turn out this way? Because Republicans and Democrats had come to believe that they could "agree to disagree" on a fix without paying a political price. Because both were at fault, nobody in particular was to blame. By the time the 2000 election rolled around, neither Clinton nor Dole would be there to answer to the voters for side-stepping the issue in the first place.

The Rest of the Story

The lowest PT elections in the sample, 1988 and 1996, are not the only ones that fit the leader-bargain category. Five additional cases, all to be found in the mid-PT category in Table 1.2, belong here as well — 1956, 1968, 1972, 1976, and 1984 — making this by far the largest of the three categories. These cases fit here for two reasons. First, as Table 1.1 showed, voters rarely achieved majority policy consensus in these years, leaving candidates relatively unconstrained by strong policy demand. Second, these new presidents made no effort, either before or after election, to enlist the support of voters to create leverage in Congress to pass legislation. As the brief review of these cases here will show, that meant that any voter policy influence would have to come from policymakers' anticipation of possible future electoral consequences and not from engagement prior to the enactment of policy.

1968

We start with 1968 because its relatively high PT numbers are misleading. This was a tumultuous year in which a growing antiwar movement made it seem likely that whoever was elected would have to find a way to disengage from Vietnam (Gould 1993). That, plus the fact of majority policy consensus and high turnout (Table 1.1), suggests that voters were driving the process. In fact, that was not the case. Broad agreement existed that resolving the Vietnam problem was the top priority, but there was also strong disagreement over how it should be done. Outside the passionate antiwar movement, mainstream public opinion gradually hardened against the demonstrators, and some people became defiantly pro-government and pro-war. By Election Day 1968, there were pockets of sharp division within the electorate. The fact of intense domestic discord over how to implement the consensus greatly reduced the pressure that voters could put on the newly elected president, Richard M. Nixon. That gave freer rein to a secretive and mistrustful man who was determined not to cede control. It invited him to play one domestic faction off against the other, much as he would eventually play the Chinese and the Soviets against one another on the international stage.

Other sources of "wiggle room" existed for Nixon as well. Table 1.1 shows that the belief in Vietnam as the most important problem facing the country barely reached majority status as the election approached, despite the antagonisms between the hawks and the doves and despite a later perception that Vietnam was an all-consuming national preoccupation at the time. Compare this bare-majority number to the much-higher consensus numbers in 1960 and 1992. Another factor was that 1968 turnout actually declined from the previous presidential election year, 1964: not what might be expected if the nation were in a high state of alarm. Last, there was no public demand for the candidates to have Vietnam plans in 1968, as there would be for candidates to have economic plans in 1992. That let candidate Nixon get away with refusing to disclose his "secret plan" to end the war (Ambrose 1989, 166).

As both candidate and as president, Nixon was notoriously reluctant to share information. "On foreign policy," wrote biographer Richard Reeves, "he tried to deal with both the people and the people's elected representatives on a 'need to know' basis. He did not trust them with the truth" (2001, 59). Once elected, Nixon simply began implementing his Vietnam policies, including a program of secret bombing of North Vietnamese troops inside the "neutral" country of Cambodia. Continuing his campaign practice, he neither publicized his ideas nor asked the public to support them; not, that is, until the antiwar movement seemed strong enough to disrupt them. The movement's growing strength alarmed him because "[h]is principal concern at home was order above all...he believed dissent and unrest, particularly among students, reduced presidential power and influence around the world" (Reeves 2001, 43). When it became clear that vocal domestic protest was encouraging North Vietnamese intransigence at the bargaining table, Nixon concluded that he had to either generate a show of public support or endure a stalemate in Vietnam. He admitted as much in his "silent majority" speech of November 3, 1969, which temporarily succeeded in convincing the world that most Americans supported the president, not the antiwar movement (Aitken 1993, 386–90). In his speech, Nixon acknowledged that the chances for success of his policies of Vietnamization and "peace with honor" would be greatly enhanced by a strong public endorsement. "The more support I can have from the American people, the sooner [my pledge to end the war] can be redeemed; for the more divided we are at home, the less likely the enemy is to negotiate at Paris...And so tonight — to you, the great silent majority of my fellow Americans — I ask for your support" (quoted in Nixon 1978, 409).

Superficially at least, Nixon sounds like a candidate in search of a policy mandate (see Chapter 4). But Nixon's plea came a year after his election, and only then as a short-term tactical move. Unlike a mandate-seeking candidate, neither Nixon's job nor his policy was at stake. He makes clear in his memoirs what was implicit in the speech: that while a show of public support would certainly be helpful, he would be sticking with his policy with or without it. "I have chosen a plan for peace. I believe it will succeed. If it does succeed, what the critics say now won't matter. If it does not succeed, anything I say then won't matter" (quoted in Nixon 1978, 409). Whatever the public did, it was always perfectly clear that Nixon would make foreign policy by himself. A divided people led by a secretive president meant that policy would be set behind the scenes and could be judged only by its consequences.

In the four remaining election seasons that fit the leader-bargain category — 1956, 1972, 1976, and 1984 —no particular links were either sought or established among voters, presidents, and policy, and there was no pronounced tendency for either the campaigns or the postelection policy debates to respond to the top priority of the electorate.

1956

The campaign of 1956 was a lackluster one, about incumbent president Dwight D. Eisenhower's health following his heart attack, until two foreign policy crises — Anglo–French military intervention at the Suez Canal, and a bloody Hungarian revolt against Soviet occupation — exploded into the headlines in the weeks before the election, making a threat of war the top public priority for a near majority (Table 1.1) and clinching a landslide reelection for the popular Eisenhower (Pach and Richardson 1991, 136).

The reelected Eisenhower did push through Congress, in March 1957, a Middle East resolution aimed at discouraging Soviet adventurism in that region. Quickly dubbed the Eisenhower Doctrine, the measure gave the president discretionary authority to furnish economic and military aid to resist Communist expansion. It might be taken as a response to the top public priority before the election, since both the public priority and the resolution dealt with the same collection of issues. But the legislative history shows that, far from being intended as a response to public concern with the threat of war in the region, it was instead Eisenhower's effort to warn the Soviet Union not to try to fill the power vacuum left by the collapse of British and French influence after the Suez debacle (Pach and Richardson 1991, 160–64).

1972

1972 saw another big drop in turnout, made worse by the passage in 1971 of the 26th Amendment giving notoriously indifferent 18-year-olds the right to vote. Vietnam was still the top pre-election issue, but by then it attracted just 27 percent support (Table 1.1). The PT ranking in Table 1.2 is 8 of 12. The circumstances were calculated to give a president — one who had just won reelection by one of the largest margins in American history, especially a brooding and resentful one like Richard Nixon — the feeling that he could do what he wished. With little public pressure to contend with, and with an electoral landslide that made him bold, what Nixon did was to suppress the evidence of his Watergate crimes. In other words, Nixon tried to sneak something big past the voters — a mistake of historic proportions that would eventually drive him from office.

In two other leader-bargain cases, 1988 and 1996, as well as in the secret Lyndon Johnson–Barry Goldwater deal of 1964 (discussed later in this chapter), sneaking big issues past the voters was the clear intent of agreements between the candidates of opposing parties. 1972 was different, however, because no secret bargain with opposition elites was involved. Nixon might have struck what would have amounted to a kind of "plea-bargain" with the Democrats who controlled Congress (i.e., publicly admitting his guilt in order to avoid impeachment). He chose instead to deny everything. This was a unilateral decision on Nixon's part. The only bargaining involved unsuccessful efforts to keep his own advisers from going public. In this sense Nixon's action, though intended to cover up an election-related felony (authorizing the break-in at the Democratic National Committee headquarters at the Watergate Building in search of information that might have aided his reelection effort), was more in the tradition of such unilateral but nonelectoral presidential deceptions as President James Polk's orchestration of the Mexican War, Teddy Roosevelt's instigation of the Panamanian Revolution, or Ronald Reagan's authorization of the Iran-Contra affair.

1976

The 1976 election was framed from the outset by public recoil from the sins of Watergate and distaste for Gerald Ford's decision to pardon Richard Nixon for his Watergate crimes. Democratic accountability was a big issue, exploited by candidate Jimmy Carter in his promise: "I'll never lie to you." By making so many promises and presenting no recognizably coherent agenda, however, Carter actually blurred the policy focus of the campaign. Carter won by just two points and neither earned nor claimed any particular policy mandate. He thought instead that he had a *process* mandate, that is, a license from the voters to change the nature of national politics and the style of national policy making (Jones 1988, 210). Part of that new approach was to define himself as a *trustee*, responsible for making decisions in the public interest as he understood it, not as a delegate who represents his constituents by embracing their policy priorities and preferences (Jones 1988, 3).

Carter's early presidency was noted for simultaneously confronting many controversial questions, thus continuing the policy blur of the campaign. He made no systematic effort to feature the high cost-of-living issue cited by 47 percent of the American people in the pre-election Gallup Poll (Table 1.1), either in the campaign or in the setting of his postelection policy priorities. Amid a hail of unrelated proposals, the closest thing to that popular priority that he submitted to Congress in the months after his election was a package designed to stimulate the sluggish economy by giving all citizens a $50 tax rebate, cutting corporate taxes by $900 million, and allocating modest increases in public works and other job-creating programs. Shortly thereafter, however, he switched his economic emphasis to preventing inflation (Kaufman 1993, 28–29). That abrupt change of direction added to public confusion about what Carter stood for, and it signaled what was to become his *modus operandi:* basing policy choice on his own analysis of the substantive merits, with less than typical and less than expected attention to either politics or public opinion.

So it was that the man who had made more concrete policy promises as a candidate than any of his predecessors (Fishel 1985, 80) never really sought to articulate an overarching purpose or sense of direction for his administration that he could invite the electorate to endorse. Instead, Carter's trusteeship approach led him to mistrust any impulse — his own or others' — to either respond to popular pressure or to cultivate public support. As often as not, he saw such options as unseemly pandering. That led him away from, not toward, policy partnerships with the American people.

1984

Last on our list of leader-bargain–anticipatory-influence cases, 1984, is remembered largely for the appearance on the Democratic ticket of the first female candidate in American history, Vice President nominee Geraldine Ferrarro. It is also remembered for its inattention to issues. Incumbent president Ronald Reagan, a candidate for reelection, set the tone. Coasting to victory amid prosperity, Reagan had no incentive to confront difficult policy questions. He chose instead to stress such vague, hopeful, and "feel good" themes as "Morning in America," and "You ain't seen nothing yet!" and to attack his opponent as an old fashioned "tax-and-spend, gloom-and-doom Democrat."

One noteworthy effort to put a real policy problem on the agenda was made by the object of those attacks, Democratic presidential nominee and former Carter vice president Walter Mondale. In a desperate effort to change the campaign dynamic and to put pressure on Reagan, he announced that whoever was elected would have to raise taxes in order to curb the out-of-control growth of the federal budget deficit. Mondale got no significant public response to his then-novel bid for what amounted to a highly specific policy mandate to reduce the deficit by increasing taxes. Instead, as some analysts saw it, he clinched his own defeat. In retrospect, that seems unlikely. Polls suggested that the hapless Mondale was headed for his eighteen-point drubbing at the hands of his popular opponent no matter what he said.

The probability is that if the electorate is not goaded by serious unhappiness with a first-term incumbent or his policies as an election approaches, then turnout will likely decline and the policy consensus will be small. Table 1.1 showed that both things came to pass in 1984. Most important, because his victory was certain, Reagan probably concluded that he had no reason to try again in 1984 what he had managed to accomplish in 1980: first to claim, and then to build, the consent of the voters for a novel policy agenda that their votes and other signs of support could help him to realize (see Chapter 4).

What the Cases Show

The two lowest PT elections, 1988 and 1996, show that the temptation to avoid campaign discussion of difficult issues is greatest when the electorate is least engaged. The capsule reviews of the elections that make up the balance of the leader-bargain category, however, show how varied are the circumstances that can reduce the likelihood that candidates and voters will reach clear understandings on what will be done before policy is enacted: divided public opinion in 1968; unexpected foreign policy crises in 1956; a paranoid president with something to hide in 1972; a moralistic president with an inhibiting attitude in 1976; and a popular incumbent with little reason to shape a policy dialogue in 1984.

The most important conclusion to this point, a conclusion supported by both the voter-driven and the leader-bargain cases, is that pre-enactment policy understandings will not emerge, indeed *cannot* emerge, without either voter pressure or presidential initiative. The comparative rarity of clear voter demand means that if such understandings are to happen at all, candidates who become new presidents must generally make them happen. The presidents in focus here chose not to do so.

Some of them might have chosen otherwise. Nixon in 1972 and Reagan in 1984, for example, both enjoyed ideal political circumstances: large victory margins over unpopular opponents with unpopular policy ideas. Both situations might well have been parlayed into policy partnerships with voters that helped create influence in Congress. For reasons of their own, however, neither of these presidents chose to make the effort. Nor did Carter in 1976, or Nixon in 1968, although their very narrow victories over much more plausible opponents would have made the task harder. Eisenhower in 1956 hoped and expected that his landslide victory would strengthen his policy hand in Congress: "If they [the voters] don't approve of what I stand for I would not understand why they voted for me" (quoted in Pach and Richardson 1991, 136). But he did not aggressively seek voter endorsement for any specific policy during his campaign, nor did he make a claim to voter policy endorsement a central part of his legislative strategy after election. Despite his landslide reelection margin, the Democrats retained control of the Congress, adding to their majorities one seat in the Senate and two in the House.

The question of why so few presidents — just three in this sample — either seek or claim prior understandings with voters is a central concern in each of the chapters to follow. We cannot end the present chapter, however, without first assessing the costs and benefits to a democratic policy-making system that, by so often side-stepping full disclosure at election time, is forced to rely heavily on the anticipation of reward or punishment once policy actions and results are disclosed.

Conclusion: Anticipatory Influence in Perspective

The democratic sufficiency of voters' power to reward and punish policy results at the next election is an article of faith among many influential political scientists (e.g., Fiorina and Peterson 1998, 14; Brody 1991, 170; Iyengar 1991, 140; Huntington 1991). This sense of sufficiency derives from the concept of democracy set forth by Joseph Schumpeter (1976), who holds that the role of voters is nothing more or less than that of choosing leaders in competitive elections. He prefaced his theory with an explicit rejection of the idea "that the democratic method is to guarantee that issues be decided and policies framed according to the will of the people" (272). For Schumpeter, the division of labor between followers and the leaders they elect "means that [followers] must refrain from instructing [leaders] about what…to do — a principle that has indeed been universally recognized by constitutions and by political theory ever since Edmund Burke's time" (295).

It is true that Schumpeter's scheme is debatable, and it has been persuasively criticized (e.g., Held 1996 191–98). In addition, there is evidence, some of which was reviewed in Chapter 1, that voters do occasionally influence policy choice directly, as well as in ways that can be called *anticipatory*. The fact remains, however, that in seven of the twelve presidential elections included in this study, Schumpeter's view of the role of the voter comes closer to reality than does the view embodied in the ideals that he rejects. Nor should the influence potential of Schumpeter's more constrained voter be dismissed as inconsequential. There is more here than meets the eye. As noted earlier, a leader's knowledge that he may be held accountable for results at the next election can indeed lead him to take anticipated voter reactions into account, which is why politicians are so reluctant to propose raising taxes, for example, or to propose tampering with Social Security, the "third rail" of American politics. That is also one reason why tax cuts are so often found in candidate platforms. Many politicians do choose or avoid policies according to whether they expect to be rewarded or punished for doing so. When this happens, voters are *ipso facto* influential. What is more, this brand of influence does not require high voter turnout or majority policy focus. It does not depend, in other words, on heroic efforts or unusual circumstances in order to function, as do the other kinds of influence described in these pages. This makes it the "default option" of American democracy and the bedrock of voter influence. In fact, anticipatory influence is properly described as the core mechanism of democratic accountability.

These virtues surely make anticipatory influence a necessity for a viable representative democracy, but to many generations of reformers the virtues have not seemed sufficient. This is because, in practice, anticipatory influence is a blunt and sometimes uncertain instrument of policy influence. For example, because accountability must await an often-distant election, the performance record is subject to expansion and is likely to be full and complex by decision time. Voters may forget particular performance episodes, or they may have difficulties prioritizing among many such episodes. In addition, there are always other more proximate influences on candidate choice, such as the force of candidate personalities,or unexpected crises, that bid to outweigh retrospective performance evaluation as the basis for choice on Election Day. For such reasons, delayed accountability can all too easily become diluted and diminished accountability.

Finally and most important, accountability can be evaded altogether. The examples of the savings and loan crisis and the Clinton-Dole Social Security agreement were cited earlier, but the most egregious example is best reported here. This was the secret bargain struck in July 1964 between incumbent president Lyndon Johnson and his Republican challenger Barry Goldwater in the run-up to the fall campaign. In essence, they agreed not to make the Vietnam War a campaign issue, and not to attack each other's position on civil rights. They wanted to avoid contentious campaign issues, and they did. In the process, however, they also prevented a real debate on two of the most important issues before the country (Bornet 1983, 109; Troy 1991). In this case, as in each of the others, democratic accountability to voters was effectively trumped.

Reformers respect anticipatory influence, and they want to leave in place the structures that promote it. For the reasons given, however, they also want to supplement it. They want to do so by figuring out how to increase the frequency with which voters help to choose policy as well as judge it. The next step in the effort to show how that might happen is to consider the final influence category: legitimizing influence.

Chapter 4
Legitimizing Influence:
The Claimed-Consent Cases

Legitimizing influence comes from respect for authority; that is, the authority of the people as expressed through elections. Respect for this authority stems from the belief that policy made by the democratically elected representatives of the people should reflect the popular will, especially when it is clearly expressed at the polls. We see this principle at work in the following example, taken from the 1964 presidential election:

> The Democratic Leadership [in Congress] seemed persuaded that the election was a signal about popular support for legislation such as Medicare, since polls showed that Medicare was a significant factor in Johnson's victory. Wilbur Mills, chairman of the Ways and Means Committee, "conceded that before the election members of Congress may not have been in step with the peoples' thinking on Medicare; but after Johnson campaigned on the issue and won by an unprecedented margin, they 'realized that people were for it for the first time.'" (quoted in Conley 2001, 90)

Legitimizing influence of a certain kind is exercised when newly elected presidents view their elections as evidence of public endorsement of their policies, and when legislators enact those policies in part because they accept the president's argument that the policies do reflect the will of the people.

There is no question that the moral authority of "the people" is the source of this kind of influence. When influence is exercised in their name, it is reasonable to conclude that the people enjoy at least nominal influence, whether they are conscious and intentional participants or not. If we are to regard their share of the influence exercised in their name as anything more than nominal, however, there must be convincing evidence that a significant percentage of the electorate actually supports the policy.

Nominal versus Real Voter Influence

Presidents who invoke the name of the people are looking for an edge in Congress. That was the presidential motive in each of the three cases to be reviewed in this chapter. Three presidents claimed the imprimatur of voters in order to increase their chances for favorable congressional action on their policy proposals. In each of these cases, claiming popular support did help to create legitimizing influence for the president. As noted in Chapter 1, however, in only one of these cases was there convincing evidence that a majority actually shared the president's priorities and endorsed the president's proposal.

Still, any time a president claims the support of the people, he creates the *potential* to boost voter influence beyond the merely nominal. Although presidents who invoke the public are mostly looking to help themselves, they are also acknowledging and publicizing the importance of public support as a source of legitimacy for the agenda and as an incentive for legislators to enact it. This gives voters a standing that they do not enjoy when, as is more common in this sample of elections, the president makes no special claim to voter support for his policies. A claim of voter support can set in motion forces that work to raise the profile of the electorate and, potentially, its real influence as well. It can, for example, mobilize pollsters to check the credibility of the new president's claim by testing and retesting public sentiment, and by publicizing the results. It can spur voters to reflect carefully on whether or not they really do support the president's plans. It can mobilize the president to mount a postelection campaign to shore up public support for legislation in anticipation of key congressional votes. And it can focus the media spotlight on the evolving state of public opinion as the legislation is debated. In theory, at least, the result could be to give the electorate an unofficial but significant role in the formulation stage of the policy process, a chance to pass widely publicized judgment on policy before it is enacted, and even a chance to influence the legislative outcome.

Such extensive influence is far from automatic, however. In fact, such influence is unlikely, because, as recent research has shown, national politicians have evolved certain standards for determining whether a president has won a policy mandate — standards that do not require concrete evidence of voter endorsement of particular legislative proposals, let alone any evidence of elaborate public participation in the shaping of policy before enactment (Conley 2001). Presidents, in other words, may wield this kind of legitimizing influence without any directly supportive voter testimony at all, because Congress has often been willing to accept a president's claim of voter endorsement of a particular piece of legislation on the basis of purely inferential evidence, such as the margin of victory. This practice lets presidents reap the political benefit of public support without proving that it actually exists for any given legislative measure, and without cultivating it on an issue-by-issue basis. When this happens, the result is to relegate voter influence to nominal status.

If we are to explore the prospects for increasing the incidence of real legitimizing influence, as we will do in the next two chapters, we must first be able to recognize when it is present and when it is not. A president creates the potential for such influence simply by claiming popular consent to the policy he proposes. That opens the door, but voters must find a way to walk through it. If they do, if a substantial number of voters (at least a sizable plurality that can plausibly represent the public, with the specific numbers dependent on case circumstances) can be shown to actually endorse or disapprove of the president's proposal as Congress prepares to vote, and if Congress then acts in concert with such substantiated expressions of the popular will, then those voters are actually influential. Presidential success has become contingent on evidence of public support. Influence is therefore assured, and voters become either *policy partners* or *saboteurs* of the president's program.

If, on the other hand, Congress acts solely on the basis of presidential claims of voter consent that are substantiated only by inferential or perceptual evidence regarded as sufficient by political elites, then voter influence is more accurately described as nominal.

Postelection Consent Claims

The process in focus here begins after Election Day, when a president refers back to his campaign to remind all concerned that he ran on an explicit policy agenda and to claim that his election victory implies public support for that agenda. Presidents Lyndon Johnson, Ronald Reagan, and George W. Bush each claimed that his election implied voter endorsement of his policies. During the campaigns, each had signaled his intent to push for dramatic, nonincremental policy changes in such areas as education, medical care, defense policy, and tax cuts. Once elected, each insisted that the voters had endorsed his bid to make these and other changes.

Table 1.1 gives gave little indication, however, of clear pre-election demand for the top policy priorities campaigned for by Johnson, Reagan, or the younger Bush. Education, Johnson's top priority, was not the highest voter priority in 1964. Tax cuts, George W. Bush's top priority, does not appear near the top of poll-tested voter priorities in Table 1.1. The table does show that the "High Cost of Living/Inflation" was the most important problem in the judgment of a strong majority in 1980. Little evidence existed before the election, however, to suggest that this implied support for Ronald Reagan's proposed solution: tax and budget cuts. In short, all three presidents lacked strong *prima facie* evidence of pre-election voter demand for what they were selling.

Nevertheless, there is nothing to prevent any newly elected president from staking a claim to voter policy support *after* the election, and then trying to persuade others — including members of Congress, journalists, and the voters themselves — to accept the validity of the claim, regardless of the state of pre-election support or the policy intentions of voters as they cast their ballots. That is exactly what George W. Bush did, for example, in 2001, despite very weak electoral credentials that supported no mandate inferences. Successful persuasion of this sort does not constitute a policy mandate, if we understand a mandate to be something that is consciously and intentionally conferred by a majority of voters as they vote, but successful postelection persuasion can indeed validate a claim to the consent of the governed to enact specific policy after the election.

Each of these presidents claimed that he had the consent of the governed for his plans and, partly for that reason, succeeded in Congress. Was the consent of the governed actually obtained? What was the potential for voter influence during the postelection, prelegislation stage, and to what extent was it realized? To address these questions, we turn to the cases.

The Johnson Advantage

The 1964 presidential campaign was in no sense a tutorial in public policy. Johnson's overall strategy was to stress consensus, to speak of the lofty goals to be served by his coming Great Society initiatives, and, especially in the early days, to paint his conservative Republican opponent, Arizona Senator Barry Goldwater, as an extreme reactionary (Bornet 1983, 104). The Johnson campaign mounted a tireless assault on Goldwater that has been described as a "masterpiece of both covert and overt negative campaigning" (Dallek 1998, 170). Goldwater's penchant for reckless overstatement eventually made Johnson's negativism seem unnecessary, however, because at no time did any poll give the Arizona senator a real chance to win the election. Accordingly, as the campaign neared its end, Johnson's advisers pressed him to return to the positive themes given their most coherent expression in his Great Society commencement speech at the University of Michigan on May 22, 1964. In more than 200 speeches over the last forty-five days of the campaign, Johnson gave voice to noble goals: "no child will go unfed and no youngster will go unschooled... [every child will have] a good teacher and every teacher good pay, and both will have good classrooms" (quoted in Bornet 1983, 103). Johnson mentioned many issues, but education was an especially pervasive theme. It was, in fact, the top priority. Johnson made that clear in a speech in Denver: "I intend to put education at the top of America's agenda" (111). Late in the race, Johnson called on the people to help him transform the nation:

I ask the American people for a mandate — not to preside over a finished program — not just to keep things going. I ask the American people for a mandate to begin. This Nation — this generation — in this hour, has man's first chance to build the Great Society (quoted in Conley 2001, 87).

After an historic election victory that added significantly to the Democratic majorities in Congress, Lyndon Johnson had amassed the strongest circumstantial claim to a policy mandate in American history. Johnson's campaign exchanges with the antigovernment, pro–states rights, anti–Social Security Republican candidate Barry Goldwater made the stark policy differences between the two men unmistakable. There was no doubt that the vast majority of voters had rejected both Goldwater and his platform. When the election was over, the evidence that spelled "mandate" to the Washington community was in place (Conley 2001, 32–50). It included a large margin of victory, sharply contrasting ideological positions, and clear policy differences between the candidates. In addition, there was a plausible inferential argument, based on the support for Johnson by demographic groups likely to benefit, that the winner's vote share and support patterns had something to do with his policy intentions. Democratic Party majorities in Congress had increased, and analysts in the media and politicians in and outside Congress were virtually unanimous that the people had in fact endorsed the Great Society in general and probably also such specifics as a war on poverty, civil rights for minorities, medical assistance for the elderly, and expanded educational opportunity for all (Bornet 1983, 117; Conley 2001, 90; Jones 1994, 154).

Few noticed, however, that the consensus regarding Johnson's mandate was based more on inferences, assumptions, and perceptions than on direct evidence of what voters did and did not care about and support. In the words of one biographer who was thoroughly familiar with the direct evidence, the only clear mandate was for "avoiding extremism of any kind at home and abroad" (Dallek 1998, 184). Johnson himself privately expressed doubts that his "smashing victory was a mandate or an unqualified national commitment to any specific legislative program" (Dallek 1998, 190), but he did see his electoral victory and ongoing popularity as an unusual opportunity to get a lot of important bills through Congress.

The most striking illustration of the gap between perception and reality involved education, Johnson's top priority and the Johnson policy proposal chosen for discussion here. A series of Gallup Polls taken roughly once a month between June 25, 1964, and October 29, 1965, posed the now-familiar question: "What do you think is the most important problem facing this country today?" In not a single one of some thirteen polls — including those taken during the intense legislative maneuvering that preceded Johnson's April 11, 1965, signing of the Elementary and Secondary Education Act — did more than 2 percent of respondents identify education as the most important problem.

Parenthetically, but still quite revealing of the true state of voter influence at the time, is the fact that the two highest poll-tested voter priorities in the months before and after the 1964 election were Vietnam and civil rights. As mentioned in the previous chapter, these were issues that Johnson and Goldwater had privately agreed to downplay during the campaign (Bornet 1983, 110).

The Elementary and Secondary Education Act of 1965

Johnson's top priority was education, which he saw as the integrative centerpiece of the Great Society. The premise was that, in order to achieve a Great Society, one had to create a War on Poverty. And in order to wage that war successfully, one needed a multifaceted attack. In addition to stimulating economic opportunity, "you had to work on education, you had to work on ill health, you had to work on Social Security, you had to work on a whole series of things....[Johnson] saw [the Great Society and the War on Poverty] as a large attack completing the Roosevelt-Truman program" (Cohen 1986, 104). Education was the centerpiece and the starting point "because it was believed that the best way to break the cycle of poverty and its associated disadvantages was through increasing the academic performance of those who were in poverty" (Hawkins 1986, 106). Johnson was determined to put "the entire power and prestige of the presidency behind the major education bill" (Bornet 1983, 123). In his 1965 State of the Union address, the president made it clear that the education proposal was to begin a program to ensure that all children would attain the fullest development of their minds and skills. Johnson sought $1.5 billion to improve preschool, elementary, secondary, and college education.

Ironically, the widespread perception that Johnson had an historic policy mandate made it possible for him to do something that he considered essential but that seemed intrinsically contradictory for a president with a mandate: to exclude the public from the preparation and the lobbying stages of the legislation. In other words, Johnson would develop the Elementary and Secondary Education Act (ESEA) legislation and push it through Congress with no campaign to publicize the contents of the legislation and no special effort to seek explicit public endorsement for it. Johnson had this option only because, as he knew well in advance of Election Day, his victory would be so overwhelming that public support would be taken for granted. If he moved quickly enough, he could be sure that the media and Congress would simply assume that the people were with him. There would be no need to seek new evidence of public support as a source of leverage in the internal congressional debate that preceded enactment.

Anticipating both a landslide victory over Goldwater and overwhelming Democratic Party dominance of the 89th Congress, Johnson had long planned to create a number of task forces that would produce legislative proposals for presentation to the new Congress in January 1965 (Graham 1981, 157). He told his Cabinet in the summer of 1964 that he was setting up fifteen task forces to develop detailed legislative proposals and that their deliberations and recommendations would be kept strictly secret. Why? Because the extra-careful Johnson was convinced that publicity would make it harder, not easier, to win legislative gains (Dallek 1998, 189). Johnson believed that the leaks that had plagued certain Kennedy administration task forces enabled opponents to sabotage the enactment of generated proposals (Graham 1981, 164). Therefore, the task forces would operate behind closed doors. "It is very important that this not become a public operation," said Johnson. "The purpose of these task forces is to come up with ideas, not to sell those ideas to the public" (quoted in Dallek 1998, 189). While Johnson spoke in generalities during the campaign about the need to press for education and other reforms, therefore, the education policy specifics being developed behind the scenes were embargoed. They would not see the light of day until January 12, 1965, when Johnson sent the bill and his education message to Congress, sparking rave media reviews (Dallek 1998, 198).

The Task Force on Education that set the outlines of the legislation, chaired by John W. Gardner, would later be regarded as a model because "[t]he history of the elementary-education bill is probably the best example of the success of the task force technique" (Graham 1981, 159). Once Gardner had submitted his report to the White House in mid November, Johnson and his top staffers transformed its broad recommendations into the legislative proposal that was sent to Congress.

Despite the fact that mobilizing new public input was not part of the legislative strategy, Johnson remained acutely aware that the legitimacy of public support was every bit as important to the bill's prospects as the internal maneuvering on Capitol Hill, and he lived in fear that public support might evaporate before he could get the measure through Congress. He repeatedly exhorted his team to redouble their efforts, fretting that he was losing support at the rate of about a million a month. He was certain that, once his opponents noticed any drop in his approval numbers, they would quickly exploit that evidence of political weakness to defeat the bill. Driven in part by that intense anxiety, Johnson and and his team maneuvered brilliantly and in record time to overcome the daunting political obstacles that had bottled up education reform for generations. To many legislators and their constituents, federal aid to education implied enforced integration, unconstitutional support of parochial schools, and excessive government control of people's lives. This entrenched opposition forced Johnson to concentrate on the "inside game" in Congress, finding ways to resolve stubborn barriers that were rooted in long-standing sectional and ideological antipathies and resentments.

It was a credit to his commitment and to a truly extraordinary legislative lobbying effort (detailed in Dallek 1998, 195–203) that he was able to do so. As a result, the education bill passed by substantial majorities. After Johnson signed it on April 11,1965, the historian Eric Goldman called it "an astonishing piece of political artistry. The Congress had passed a billion dollar law, deeply affecting a fundamental institution of the nation, in a breathtaking 87 days" (quoted in Dallek 1998, 200).

Public Influence

What, finally, can we conclude about the nature and the extent of voter influence? The interpretive mandate tradition described by Conley (2001) ensured that Johnson's extraordinary margin of victory over an unpopular opponent would give this wily legislative politician enough leverage, even on an extraordinarily complex issue like education, to trump the opposition to his policy. The consensus was that the voters had helped make possible one of the most productive legislative records in presidential history. Voters had indeed helped by giving Johnson an overwhelming election victory. Indeed, it was the largest margin of victory among the 12 elections considered here (Table 4.1). But did they actually support the education policy?

Johnson enjoyed 67 percent approval in the Gallup Poll in the week preceding the signing of ESEA (Edwards 1990, 42). Even so, the Gallup Poll numbers for "the most important problem" on March 23, 1965, less than three weeks before the bill signing, put "education and related needs" at just 1 percent (Gallup, 1965). If education was Johnson's top priority, it was certainly not the public's. That distinction was reserved for civil rights, at 46 percent, followed by Vietnam at 23 percent.

TABLE 4.1 MARGINS OF VICTORY 1956–2000 ELECTIONS

Election Year	Winner	Point Spread	Margin
1956	Eisenhower	57–42	15
1960	Kennedy	49–49	.01
1964	Johnson	61–38	23
1968	Nixon	43–42	.07
1972	Nixon	61–38	23
1976	Carter	50–48	2
1980	Reagan	51–41	10
1984	Reagan	59–41	18
1988	Bush	53–46	7
1992	Clinton	43–37	6
1996	Clinton	49–41	8
2000	Bush	æ	æ

Despite the low priority they assigned to education, however, voters might have been willing to express support for a popular president's education bill just because they knew he wanted it. Were they? One of the few available polls that specifically asked about the public's support of the education initiative during this period suggested that the answer was "yes." In April, the month when Johnson signed the ESEA bill, Harris Poll interviewers asked, "From what you know or have heard, do you tend to favor or oppose what [President Lyndon Johnson] has been doing on Federal aid to education?" Seventy-seven percent were in favor, with 23 percent opposed (Roper Center 1995, 0245688). In February, however, a Gallup Poll had asked how satisfied respondents were with "[t]he public school system in your town?" The answers help to explain why education attracted so few "top priority" mentions. Twenty-six percent described themselves as "Extremely well satisfied;" 37 percent as "Considerably well satisfied;" 23 percent as "Somewhat satisfied;" and only 11 percent as "Not at all satisfied" (Roper Center 1990, 0038892). Finally, another February Gallup Poll asked "What things do you like about President Johnson?" The largest plurality — 17 percent — identified "his personality and character." None of Johnson's policies fared nearly as well. For example, "Domestic policy handling in general and handling of specific domestic programs" garnered 5 percent. "Program for aid to education" was mentioned by just 2 percent (Roper Center 1989a, 0039542). Education had not been mentioned at all in a Harris Poll, taken a month earlier, that asked the same question.

Piecing these poll results together, the picture that emerges is of a public with priorities other than education, but also a public that, at the time, was favorably disposed toward President Johnson. For that reason, rather than because of any urgent belief that the face of education in America needed changing, people were willing to go along with what the president wanted — up to a point. In response to another February Gallup Poll, people made it clear that if there were to be increased expenses, 49 percent wanted the federal government to pick up the tab for the "expectable increased tax burden for education costs," and just 42 percent were willing to have the states do so (Roper Center 1989b. 003956).

Whatever their motives and however low the priority they assigned to education, nevertheless most voters did support a new federally financed education bill. By the time the highly supportive Harris Poll emerged, their expression of support scarcely mattered. Public support had already achieved the status of a "given." It had not been seriously in question since Election Day. The evolving state of public opinion on the education debate was therefore of little interest on Capitol Hill or in the White House; news organizations saw no reason to include fresh assessments of it in the unfolding legislative story; and pollsters rarely asked about it. This left voters with no role in the ongoing debate and little chance to have a say on the merits, whether on the shape of education or any other Great Society policy being legislated in their name. The Johnson case makes it hard not to conclude that overwhelming presidential election victories are more likely to *diminish* than to *increase* the chances for real voter policy influence.

The Reagan Television Campaign

Table 1.1 shows that economic issues were the top concern of 60 percent of probable voters just before the 1980 election. In fact, Gallup Polls dating from March 1980 through October 1981 show a consistent pattern of majority voter concern with the combination of inflation, the high cost of living, and high prices, with the percentages reaching 70 in the two polling months following Republican candidate Ronald Reagan's election (Gallup Poll Archives, March 1980–October 1981). In focusing his campaign on economic issues, Reagan was clearly more in sync with voter priorities than Lyndon Johnson had been. Reagan's multiyear "supply side" tax cut proposal — the centerpiece of his campaign and, together with his proposed budget cuts, our focus here — was an outgrowth of his endorsement of past plans offered by Republican Senators Jack Kemp and William Roth, coupled with the promise of significant budget cuts. Reagan also made campaign issues of President Jimmy Carter's failed economic policies and his weak leadership. The Carter criticisms in particular — more so than the policy proposals — resonated with voters. As the election year dawned, seventy percent thought that the country had gotten seriously off track. By October 1980 voters also thought, by a two-to-one margin, that Reagan was a stronger leader than Carter.

For his part, President Carter sought to deflect attention from the troubled economy and toward Reagan's inexperience, especially in foreign affairs. He painted Reagan as a dangerous choice in the nuclear age and as so far to the right on most domestic-policy issues that he was well outside the American political mainstream. Although many voters did come to believe that Carter was better able to keep the nation out of war, and although the number of undecided voters remained unusually high until just days before the election, in the end more voters proved to be unhappy with Carter than fearful of Reagan.

Reagan's unexpected ten-point victory over the unpopular Carter, combined with the Republican capture of the Senate and notable gains in the House of Representatives, "led to expectations that the Reagan program would be put into effect" (Jones 1994, 220). Exit polls showed that the most common reasons given for voting for Reagan were a desire for change and dissatisfaction with economic conditions, especially inflation. Many saw the message of the election as the rejection of Jimmy Carter rather than the endorsement of the Reagan economic agenda. Still, "the common wisdom of journalists and politicians was that Americans were asking for significant changes in economic policy" (Conley, 2001, 105; 92).

The 1981 Economic Recovery Tax Act and the 1981 Omnibus Budget Reconciliation Act

Reagan, eager to seize the moment, had met with Republican leaders in Congress before the election, and together they had issued a five-point "Capitol Compact" that featured tax and spending cuts. Once elected, both president and congressional Republicans were ready to hit the ground running. In a news conference two days after the election, Reagan signaled his intentions: "I expect to move as swiftly as possible. I think [the economic program] is the most important thing, I think it was the issue of the campaign; I think it is what the American people told us with their votes they wanted. And so we'll move instantly on that" (quoted in Conley 2001, 106).

The circumstantial case for a mandate seemed compelling to most observers. Reagan had campaigned on economic policy, had won a large Electoral College victory, had attracted many disaffected Democrats, and had amassed votes in every region of the country. Journalists and politicians agreed that Reagan had won a mandate. Nevertheless, there was little evidence that voters had intentionally endorsed anything more specific than unhappiness with Jimmy Carter and with economic conditions.

The case against the mandate interpretation included the lingering uncertainty of the outcome as people struggled with their ambivalence over the choice between Carter and Reagan. Polls taken on the weekend before the election showed the race too close to call, with the turn to Reagan coming only in the last two days. A January 1981 *Time* magazine poll that asked a national sample of voters to interpret the meaning of Reagan's ten-point victory found that 62 percent felt the election was "a rejection of President Carter," and only 24 percent labeled it "a mandate for more conservative policies." Surprisingly, only 30 percent of self-described conservatives, and 34 percent of those identifying themselves as Republicans, called the election a mandate (reported in Conley 2001, 193, note 156). Charles O. Jones reaches similar conclusions: "Analysis of survey data following the [1980] election cast serious doubt on whether voters were *consciously* awarding Ronald Reagan a mandate for his conservative, antigovernment proposals. Many voters were rejecting Carter, not necessarily approving Reagan" (1994, 152; emphasis added). Still, "members of Congress, bolstered by near uniformity in mass media accounts and by partially engineered constituency pressure, clearly were persuaded...that the president was riding high" (Greenstein, 1983:174).

The Legislative Campaign

The election over, Reagan and his staffers turned to the business of pressuring Congress to pass his budget and tax cuts. Reagan immediately began an intense and personal behind-the-scenes lobbying effort. In his first one hundred days in office, he held some sixty-nine meetings with legislators, in which some 467 members took part. He cultivated southern Democrats, known as "Boll Weevils," and he even developed a warm personal relationship with Democratic House Speaker Thomas P. (Tip) O'Neill. Reagan aides knew that the president could be persuaded to call any legislator at any time, and they frequently asked him to do so (Cannon 1982, 333–34).

Despite his electoral success, Reagan had important political weaknesses. Unlike Johnson, he did not enjoy full partisan control of Congress. Republicans controlled the Senate, but the president confronted a House of Representatives controlled by Democrats with little sympathy for his conservative economic plans. That meant Reagan could not risk relying entirely on his perceptual mandate and an intense "inside-the-beltway" lobbying campaign, as Johnson had done. He would have to bludgeon at least some Democrats into submission from the outside in order to win in the House. He would need to generate new and convincing evidence that the public not only supported his economic agenda but also wanted the Congress to enact it.

In a series of televised speeches, the new president made it clear that he was inviting the public into the game. The hope was to generate fresh evidence of popular support, timed to appear at key moments during the legislative debate, which would send a not-so-subtle warning that opposing the president's program could prove to be costly in the next election.

In the first television address on February 5, 1981, Reagan said the nation faced "the worst economic mess since the Great Depression," and offered his tax and budget cuts as a solution. On February 18, he addressed the nation again before a joint session of Congress, adding tax- and budget-cut details. With the congressional debate over the tax and budget cuts under way, Reagan's personal approval polls declined slightly — a factor his supporters rationalized as spending political capital to press a controversial set of proposals. Even so, an *ABC News/Washington Post* poll released on February 20, 1981, showed that 73 percent approved of the income-tax cut at the heart of the Reagan program, while 72 percent expressed approval for the spending cuts (Roper Center, 1989c: 0006883; 0006881).

Approval of Reagan's performance rebounded after an assassination attempt in late March, and support for his tax- and budget-cut plans stayed strong at 64 and 60 percent respectively in a March 29 *ABC News/ Washington Post* poll (Roper Center, 1989d: 0007231; 0007229). On April 28, 1981, the recently wounded president made another nationally televised speech, again before a joint session of Congress. In preparation for that appearance, Reagan's political handlers had arranged for the Republican National Committee to "send party officials to the South over the Easter recess to stimulate grass-roots pressure on those Democratic representatives whose districts had gone heavily for Reagan in the November election. Party officials were also sent to Ohio where Republican representatives were reportedly wavering" (Kernell 1997, 146). In conjunction with the grass-roots lobbying, the April 28 speech apparently helped to tip the balance of votes in the Democratically controlled House of Representatives; shortly thereafter, the general budget resolution outlining the Reagan blueprint for spending cuts passed by a large margin. Said one representative of his Democratic Party colleagues who supported the resolution: "They say they're voting for it because they're afraid" (quoted in Goldman, 1981, 40). An April 22 *ABC News/Washington Post* poll showed approval of the spending cuts holding at 64 percent (Roper Center 1989e: 0007401).

In the next phase of the legislative process, a struggle to win passage of the specific spending cuts needed to implement the general budget resolution, Reagan again used public pressure. This time it took the form of television interviews and orchestrated congressional contacts by business allies from the relevant congressional districts. The aim was to beat back a Democratic effort to kill the spending cuts by having the appropriations for individual programs voted on separately, giving opponents greater leverage. Reagan, with the help of budget director David Stockman's knowledge of the House's procedural rules, succeeded in forcing a single, up-or-down vote, which resulted in the passage of the Reagan budget.

The fight in the House for the tax cuts was closer and more controversial than the budget battle had been, even though public support for the tax cut had been above 60 percent since February. (A May 19 *NBC News/Associated Press* poll, for example, showed public approval for the tax cut at 64 percent; Roper Center 1989f, 0084811.) Reagan still managed to prevail, in late July, with the support of the same coalition of Republicans and southern Democrats that had carried the budget vote. The victory required another period of intense bargaining, however, leveraged by another key television address, on July 27, in which the president urged his listeners to contact their senators and representatives to tell them that the people supported the Reagan proposal (Kernell 1997, 150).

In the end, the Democratically controlled House of Representatives passed the Omnibus Budget Reconciliation (spending cut) bill by a margin of 238 to 195, with most Democrats in opposition. The margin in the Republican Senate was 88 to 10, with 37 Democrats in support. On this measure, as on the Economic Recovery Tax Act, three factors were decisive: Republican solidarity in both houses; the crucial votes supplied by the Boll Weevil Democrats in the House; and a spirit of resignation among House Democratic leaders (Palmer and Sawhill 1984, 49–52). When the tax- and spending-cut bills were finally signed in August, public support was still firmly in place. A May 11, 1981, Gallup Poll had shown that 56 percent believed that the total amount of spending cuts proposed by Reagan was either "about right" or "too low;" an August 17 Gallup Poll showed that 64 percent of a national telephone sample still favored the tax-cut program (Roper Center 1989g, 0029696; 1989h: 0029899).

Public Influence

Reagan very likely would have gotten most Republican votes without the need to mobilize public opinion, but the Democrats were another story. They had to feel public pressure in order to move toward the president, and Reagan was masterful at creating this pressure. His television appeals had much to do with sustaining a consistent pattern of strong public support for tax and budget reductions that spanned the months of February through August, 1981, when the bill was signed. That pattern of support, apparent in the previously cited polls, helped Reagan to hold the Boll Weevil Democrats, and it also helped to provoke a loss of morale among House Democratic leaders. These proved to be the decisive factors. As one reporter put it: "Lawmakers believed their constituents supported that program and they were afraid that Mr. Reagan could galvanize that support through an adroit use of television and punish any dissidents at the polls" (Roberts 1982, 13).

Such feelings were reinforced not only by public-opinion telephone surveys, but also by "the waves of mail, telegrams, and phone calls that overwhelmed Congress after each presidential address. According to one estimate, Reagan's public appeals generated about fifteen million more letters than normally flowed into congressional mailrooms each session" (Kernell 1997, 151). That was enough to convince the congressional majorities that passed the legislation that they were implementing the public's wishes. No less an authority than the leading opposition figure rendered the final verdict: "I can read Congress," said Democratic House Speaker Tip O'Neill shortly before the vote. "They go with the will of the people, and the will of the people is to go along with the President. I've been in Congress a long time. I know when you fight and when you don't" (quoted in Stockman 1986, 174).

In contrast to the Johnson case, Reagan had generated explicit evidence of public support for his program, and it proved to be instrumental in securing passage of path-breaking legislation. It was legislation that the majority had not endorsed in any specific way on Election Day, but Reagan's postelection campaign enabled him to generate fresh and compelling evidence that a strong majority endorsed his tax and budget cuts. Proving that he had closed the sale with the American people clearly helped him pull together enough votes to close the sale in Congress.

Real and Intentional Influence

By the definition given earlier, this was real voter influence. The citizen majorities that repeatedly endorsed the Reagan program after the 1980 election convinced many Democratic Party legislators, who would otherwise have voted against the president, to vote with him.

The Reagan case also introduces another important feature of voter influence — *intentionality* — that will figure in the argument presented in Chapter 5. It is clear that those who responded to pollsters with expressions of support for Reagan's program were truly in favor of it, and they also influenced some key swing congressional votes. What is uncertain, however, is how many of those contacted by pollsters actually had in mind the intent to influence the legislative outcome as they expressed their support.

The estimated 15 million extra letter writers who were moved to respond to Reagan's call to contact their representatives — about 17 percent of the 1980 vote total and about 35 percent of the number that voted for Reagan — were different. They clearly *did* have the intent to influence the outcome in mind. That intent and the direct congressional lobbying it produced made them conscious, deliberate, and active policy partners with the president.

The Policy Partnership Difference

Why did a public that was skeptical of the Reagan economic program before the election — a public that might just as easily have rejected Reagan's postelection appeals for support — instead end up offering a ringing endorsement? The "Great Communicator's" televised appeals undoubtedly had something to do with it, but it is also the case that Reagan's proposals were responsive to what a strong majority saw as the most important problem facing the nation — something that was not true of the Johnson proposal. People wanted action on the economy, and after the election Reagan was the only person in a position to offer it. That is why opinion about Reagan's specific proposals moved from ambivalence to support.

It is noteworthy, too, that a strong popular majority shared Reagan's economic priority before he was elected, independently of his influence. That shared objective signaled a special potential for the kind of policy partnership that emerged. What made public influence in this case *real* and not merely *nominal* was the fact that the public's collective decision to support Reagan's particular economic fix was crucial to its success in Congress, as well as the fact that public opposition could have killed the program by emboldening its Democratic opponents.

The Bush Road Show

The 2000 presidential campaign and election was distinctive in many ways, not least because it produced a president who managed to win early legislative approval for an eleven-year, $1.35 trillion tax cut, the largest since

Reagan's some twenty years earlier. That president — George W. Bush — recorded this achievement within seven months of an election in which he lost the popular vote after failing to generate more than lukewarm public support for the signature policy proposal on which the legislation was based: a ten-year $1.6 trillion across-the-board tax-cut plan. Despite some evidence of public ambivalence, Bush — from the earliest stages of the presidential campaign to the late stages of the legislative struggle — consistently claimed that the people were in favor of his tax cut (Calmes 2001, A9). Bush had one important asset that Reagan did not have: partisan control, albeit narrow, of both houses of Congress. His electoral credentials were so weak, however, that — unlike Johnson but like Reagan — he resolved to cultivate public support beyond Election Day right up until the day the tax cut was enacted.

Context

Bush started from a position of weakness. He didn't just lack the electoral credentials enjoyed by Johnson and Reagan, he also lacked other supportive circumstances. There was, in the first place, little impassioned public demand, either before or after the election, for nonincremental change of any kind, let alone for Bush's extraordinarily ambitious policy agenda; this included not only his signature tax-cut proposal, but also a significant education proposal, a contentious missile defense shield proposal, an unprecedented faith-based initiative, and many other controversial measures.

A second disadvantage for Bush in comparison to Johnson and Reagan was that his opponent, Vice President and Democratic Party nominee Al Gore, took policy positions that were generally more popular than his own. A poll released by the Pew Research Center for The People and the Press on November 1, 2000, showed, for example, that Gore had solid leads over Bush on making prescription drugs more affordable for seniors, Social Security, Medicare and health care; Gore also had leads, albeit narrower ones, on maintaining the economy, world affairs, and education. Bush, on the other hand, had clear leads on only two issues: defense policy and reducing partisan conflict (Pew Research Center, November 1, 2000). Over the course of the campaign, Bush did manage to gain some ground against Gore on the tax issue. Pew Center polls between March and mid October 2000 show a Bush increase (from 40 to 45 percent) and a Gore decline (from 44 to 41 percent) on the question of which candidate would "do the best job of dealing with taxes." The political value of the shift was uncertain, however, since taxes were never a high voter priority. In five consecutive Gallup Polls — one well before the election (April 2000) and four after, in the months (January, March, April, and May) leading up to the June 2001 presidential signing of the tax-cut legislation — not once did the percentage of voters identifying taxes as "the most important problem facing the nation" exceed low single digits (Gallup Poll News Service, 2001).

A third disadvantage for Bush was that, unlike Reagan, he had to pitch his tax cut during good economic times. He did not have the assistance of widespread economic pain or a tax revolt to suppress doubts and firm up support. As Table 1.1 showed, there was no majority consensus on the most important problem facing the nation near Election Day in 2000. The largest plurality, a scant 18 percent, put education, not taxes, in the top spot.

Fourth, there was no wholesale electoral rejection of Bush's opponent, Al Gore, in 2000, as there had been of Barry Goldwater and Jimmy Carter in 1964 and 1980, respectively. Gore actually won the popular vote, which denied Bush any margin of victory to point to. That left Bush to test the dubious but intriguing proposition that he could enlist the help of the electorate (which had just given more votes to his opponent and was skeptical of his tax plan) to persuade Congress to endorse his plan, and that he could do it without anything approaching the electoral achievements or the circumstantial advantages that lent credence to the mandate claims of his two most successful predecessors.

The Tax-Cut Decision

In the face of all these disadvantages, why did George W. Bush decide to place such a high priority on a controversial tax-cut proposal? Simply, he had campaigned extensively for it and for the rest of his agenda, he believed that he was elected because of the power of the ideas reflected in that agenda, and he felt that the best way to establish his credibility with the American people was to do exactly what he said he would do, starting with his tax-cut proposal.

He started with tax cuts because an early move on taxes would send a signal to economic conservatives in the Republican Party. They would be encouraged to feel that, despite his father's notorious betrayal of his famous "read my lips, no new taxes" campaign promise, the younger Bush could be trusted. Bush's willingness to champion their most cherished ideological cause, despite its obvious political liabilities, would do more to overcome the hesitancy of conservatives to support him than anything else Bush could have done. In fact, it gave him instant credibility with the most powerful wing of his party and branded him as a conservative Republican in a way his just as highly touted education reform proposal, with its intentionally bipartisan appeal, could not do. That helped to create, for Bush, the incalculably important security of a strong and contented political base.

In addition, Bush saw the tax issue as a way to demonstrate political courage, which he believed would win him respect and would burnish his leadership credentials. This could help to convert the skeptical public reaction to his tax plan from a liability into a virtue, with appeal even to some who disagreed with him on policy grounds. It did this by letting him "prove his claim that he is a politician who puts principle ahead of polls and popularity" — a point of great personal pride that he emphasized throughout the presidential campaign (Bruni 2001, S4, 16).

Finally, Bush was encouraged by late-breaking and unexpected developments like ever-larger budget surplus projections, comments in favor of the tax cut by Federal Reserve Chairman Alan Greenspan (Stevenson 2001a, A1), similar comments by congressional Democrats, and emerging signs of an economic slowdown. Once he was installed in the White House, these factors, together with growing pressure from within his party to seize the opportunity, pushed him to make the tax proposal the top legislative priority and therefore a defining test of his ability as president to get results. The final decision was to "go for broke," to try to get the full $1.6 trillion, ten-year tax cut immediately, while the Republicans still controlled both houses of Congress and while Bush was still in his honeymoon period with the public.

Strategy

Bush's prospects for getting anything resembling his $1.6 trillion proposal through Congress remained uncertain, however. The circumstances of his election and public skepticism about the tax cut led Bush and his advisers to conclude that even though he enjoyed narrow Republican majorities in both houses of Congress, he could not afford to rely exclusively on congressional lobbying, as Johnson had done, to win passage of his top legislative priority. Because everyone knew that a president who had lost the popular vote had no electoral mandate for anything, Bush would have to embrace, with some modifications, the Reagan approach. He would have to try to create some mandate-like momentum for his tax cut after the election. National television addresses, buttressed by one or two forays into the heartland by surrogates, would not be enough. Bush would have to barnstorm the country like a presidential candidate and personally exhort the people to help him persuade the Congress to act. The strategy was to "[h]ave the president visit key states around the country, where he could put maximum pressure on wavering members of Congress." The effort would dominate his first one hundred days in office (Sanger and Lacey 2001, A1).

The Campaign

Bush launched his postelection public-relations campaign to sell the tax cut in early February 2001, with a White House event that reprised a favorite 2000 campaign tactic: showcasing "tax families" of middle-class people whose financial profiles made the case that the Bush tax cut was better for them than the Democratic alternative (Bruni 2002, 102). Despite the fact that the provisions of the Bush proposal could easily be shown to benefit the well-to-do far more than all others, the president sought to play up the benefits aimed at the middle class. The presence of a group of middle-class families at the White House, and the president's introduction of one such couple — Paul and Debbie Peterson — who would gain $1,100 per year from his plan, according to Bush, made that showcase message crystal clear (Schlesinger and Heinauer, 2001, A28). The intent, of course, was the same as it had been during the campaign: to blunt the attacks of his "favor the rich" critics. Bush also sought to broaden the tax-cut measure's appeal to middle-income voters and to put members of Congress on notice that he would be calling on precisely those voters, the largest voting bloc in the electorate, to help him persuade the Congress to pass his tax-cut plan.

Speeches and Travels

In a nationally televised speech before Congress on February 27, 2001, the new president made the case that his tax cut was sensible and affordable, and he invited both Congress and the American people to enlist in the effort to enact it. He argued that America deserved and could afford to benefit personally from the large budget surplus. The budget he would propose would "fund our priorities," pay down the national debt, and still leave room for $1.6 trillion in tax relief, a figure he described as "not arbitrary" and "just right." Anticipating opposition, he said: "As we debate, let us remember whose money this surplus is," vowing to "return the money to the people who earned it." "The surplus is not the government's money," reiterated Bush shortly thereafter in Omaha, Nebraska, on the first of what would be many trips around the country to sell his plan. "The surplus is the people's money. And I'm here to ask you to join me in making that case to any federal official you can find" (quoted in Stevenson, 2001b: A1).

With the Washington segment of the public-relations campaign behind him, Bush "took to the road to sell the tax cut in campaign-style trips to states of Senate Democrats who may be vulnerable in 2002" (Mitchell 2001, A12). The main purpose of the president's travels came into sharp focus with the House of Representative's passage, on March 9, of the cornerstone component of the Bush plan: a $958 billion across-the-board tax cut. The measure passed on a near-party-line vote, with 219 Republicans and just 10 Democrats in support. House Ways and Means Committee Chairman William M. Thomas (R-Calif.) struck early in the ideologically polarized House, forcing the measure through even before the budget resolution had been agreed on (Wilson Center News Digest 2002). House Democrats protested his hardball tactics, but, for the first time since the Eisenhower administration, a Republican Speaker (Dennis Hastert) was able to deliver a victory on a Republican president's signature issue.

Given the narrow but zealous Republican majority, a favorable House vote had been expected, but a Senate split evenly down the middle on party representation posed a much more formidable political challenge.

The hope was that the president, bolstered by the momentum of a first-round victory in the House, could use his persuasive charm in carefully selected locations to put pressure on enough key senators to help make the difference when the time came to vote.

There followed a thirteen-state campaign — the real opening of the postelection tax-cut road show — to mobilize public pressure on vulnerable Democrats and fence-sitting Republicans. Seven of the states had incumbent Democratic senators who sought reelection in 2002 after narrow 1996 victories or who faced difficult reelection campaigns for other reasons. Three states had Republican incumbents who either faced tough competition or who had expressed reservations about Bush's plan. At his many stops, which also included the hometowns of high-profile tax cut opponents — House Minority Leader Richard Gephardt (D-Mo.) and Senate Minority Leader Tom Daschle (D-S.D.) — Bush exhorted his audiences, as he put it in one speech, "to e-mail some of the good folks from the U.S. Senate from your state. If you like what you hear, why don't you just give them a call or write them a letter and let them know that the people are speaking?"

Each of the stops featured campaign-style hoopla, including bands, banners, and "$1.6 trillion — It's just right" balloons (Toedtman and Povich 2001, A19). By April 6, the date the Senate passed a budget resolution that included a compromise $1.2 trillion tax-cut provision, Bush had visited some twenty-two states in his aggressive effort to rally public opinion to his side (Stevenson 2001c, A9). The effort expanded to twenty-six states by April 29, a modern travel record for the start of a presidency (Sanger and Lacey 2001, A1). In all, Bush spent some thirty days away from the White House, selling his program in the states.

It is noteworthy that the national press corps did not cover Bush's travels extensively, but local media gave it abundant attention (Sanger and Lacey 2001, A1), presumably intensifying the effects of Bush's salesmanship on local audiences. No comprehensive record of the number of congressional contacts prompted by Bush's appeals has been assembled, but the staff person responsible for constituent mail in the Washington office of Senator Max Baucus, (D., Mont.), one of the politically vulnerable Democrats whom Bush considered special targets of opportunity, reported that the issue generating the largest volume of constituent contacts in 2001 was the Bush tax cut proposal (Susan Powell, personal communication, June 7, 2002). The fact that Bush asked virtually every audience he faced to make such contacts suggests that the Baucus experience was not unusual. It is likely that many in Bush's audiences responded by e-mailing, writing, or telephoning their representatives in Washington.

Supplemental Lobbying

Bush's road show was also supplemented throughout by an unprecedented effort by some twenty business groups that financed advertising, direct-mail, and telephone campaigns to reach hundreds of thousands of people who were exhorted to contact their representatives and demand that they vote for the Bush plan. Knowing that the vote would be closer in the Senate than it had been in the House, and that both Democratic and Republican votes would be necessary for success, Bush also extensively lobbied key senators, ferrying them to and from Washington, D.C., on Air Force One and listening to their "wish lists" as they engaged in "private give and take." Most of the direct Washington lobbying, however, was shouldered by Vice President Dick Cheney and Budget Director Mitch Daniels. The message invariably pressed on sympathetic legislators was that they should subordinate their many disagreements with the specifics of the tax-cut proposal in the interests of ensuring that the new president be able to establish his leadership by notching a legislative victory.

Surrogate Hardball

The Bush team's effort to enlist the public to put pressure on legislators was not limited to the president's own program of speeches, appearances, and radio addresses. It also featured some rather blunt and highly specific pressure applied by Bush surrogates to wavering senators in states with electorates known or believed to be especially sympathetic to the president and/or his party. For example, Mitch Daniels traveled to Nebraska, the home state of wavering Democratic senator Ben Nelson, who had won his seat narrowly in a state that Bush carried in 2000 and that Bush visited more than once during the tax-cut campaign. There, in an effort to stigmatize Nelson with Republican voters whose support Nelson needed for political survival, Daniels attacked him for caving into pressure from "Democratic elders" in the Senate and voting against the Bush version of the budget resolution in April. Nelson voted for the trimmed-down, $1.35 trillion version of the Bush tax cut in May (Barone 2001, 929).

Massachusetts native Andrew Card, the president's chief of staff, hit the airwaves in Republican Senator Jim Jeffords's home state of Vermont, pressing the maverick Republican senator to "give the president a chance." The result: Jeffords voted for the compromise $1.35 trillion tax cut, giving Bush what was interpreted as a victory, "even as [Jeffords] announced he was leaving the Republican Party" (Barone 2001, 1548).

Bush's use of targeted public pressure created some resentment among politically vulnerable members of Congress. In the end, however, they had little choice but to submit. Such pressure was a major factor in winning votes on both sides of the aisle, but especially among the twelve Democratic senators and twenty-eight Democratic members of the House who sided with the president.

The Public Responds

The Bush tax cut proposal may have been the most heavily polled presidential initiative to date. Roper Center online records for polls tracking the entry "tax cut" between January 1 and August 1, 2001, yield a list of 305 items, far more than is available for either the Johnson or Reagan initiatives. What these items show can be summarized as follows. First, in each of the five months from Bush's inauguration in January to congressional approval of the legislation in May, the Bush tax-cut proposal received majority or plurality approval in every poll. The tax-cut campaign undoubtedly had something to do with this. The average level of approval in thirteen national telephone surveys spread across the five months was 54 percent. A review of the entire period uncovered no poll in which opponents of the tax cut were a majority or a plurality. Furthermore, majorities repeatedly stated that they believed the tax cut would help rather than hurt the economy.

The second set of findings was less favorable to the president. As shown in the series of Gallup Polls cited earlier, at no time during this period did a significant percentage of the sampled national public place a high priority on tax cuts. By early March, to cite another example, a *Wall Street Journal/NBC News* poll showed that although a healthy majority, 57 percent, favored the Bush proposal, only 14 percent named federal taxes as the most important *economic* issue — compared with 35 percent who picked energy prices (Calmes 2001, A9).

More troubling still from the administration's perspective, important caveats and qualifications consistently surfaced, in these and most other polls on the tax question taken during the winter and spring of 2001, to dilute the political value of the majority support that President Bush had managed to attract. For example, many polls found that majorities and pluralities would have preferred a *smaller* tax cut than the one Bush proposed. And poll after poll signaled the public's conviction that the Bush tax cut favored the rich. Most implied or asserted that this was a flaw that should be corrected, either to make better use of the money or to serve the value of fairness. As one example, 52 percent in the March *Wall Street Journal/NBC News* poll said that tax cuts should be aimed at middle- and lower-income Americans rather than the wealthy, and should leave enough revenue for reducing the federal debt and funding priorities like education. In a February Pew poll, a large majority of those who wanted the surplus used to fix entitlement programs — 79 percent — said that the president's tax cut unfairly benefited some, most notably the rich, more than others (Pew Online Reports 2001, 2).

Many polls in the Roper collection included questions asking people to choose between a tax cut and investment in Social Security and Medicare reform. Despite strong evidence of majority endorsement for the Bush tax cut, majorities also consistently, if paradoxically, said they favored using the budget surplus to shore up these entitlement programs rather than to finance that tax cut. They continued to say so after the passage of the tax cut, whose support finally dropped below a majority. For example, a June 2001 *New York Times/CBS News* poll found that only 28 percent favored using the federal budget surplus for a tax cut, while 64 percent said it would have been better used to preserve Social Security and Medicare (Berke and Elder 2001, A1). An *ABC News/Washington Post* poll released on June 3 asked: "What would have been your own preference — to have this tax cut or to have the Federal Government spend more on domestic programs such as education, health care and Social Security?" Sixty-three percent opted for more domestic spending; only 33 percent stuck with the tax cut (Roper Center Public Opinion Online 2001, 0382712). Something like "buyer's remorse" over the tax cut seemed to be settling in.

How Bush Did It

The Bush case is unique for being mixed. Bush was politically the weakest of the three presidents in this sample and the most in need of public help. He got selective citizen help in key states to pressure swing Senate voters to pass his tax cut. When polls showed that the public at large wanted changes, however, Bush did not budge. He stuck to his guns and got most of what he wanted anyway, signing the Economic Growth and Tax Relief Reconciliation Act of 2001 into law in early June (Sanger 2001, A8). How did such a politically weak president manage to succeed without any deference to public criticism? By mobilizing public pressure on vulnerable legislators, as we have seen, but also by taking advantage of muddled public-opinion polls that mixed both support and criticism. This made it possible for him to dismiss the polls as confused and meaningless and thus not to be taken seriously. He was aided by the fact that tax policy was a low priority for voters, generating little passion either way. With the polls at least rhetorically discredited, Bush had a rationale for ignoring the public criticisms of his tax cut that they revealed. He also had a plausible reason for basing his claim on public support entirely on the fact of his election.

More frequently than any new president since Reagan, Bush reminded the country that he had run on an agenda. He repeatedly asserted his belief that because he had won the election after disclosing his plans during the campaign, he had earned the right, not just to assume the presidency but also to pass his policy agenda. The implication was that the certification of election by the people — never mind the loss of the popular vote or the controversy — was a far more important endorsement of his policies than anything the polls might say. And he made it clear to every audience that he felt it entitled him, not just to a respectful hearing, but to congressional support for his tax cut proposal.

Given the controversial circumstances of his election and the muddled state of public opinion, this was strategically bold and almost certainly beneficial to his cause. It helped him to shift congressional attention away from his electoral shortcomings and onto his status as a legitimate president with an agenda. And it encouraged senators and representatives to minimize the importance of widespread poll evidence of public ambivalence toward his tax-cut proposal. To the extent that members of Congress found Bush persuasive, public reservations were set aside and public influence was diminished. In short, Bush claimed and used the consent of the governed on his own terms. For that reason, and also because the measure that he signed into law contained much that poll majorities clearly did not want, voter clout in the Bush tax cut case, though including an element of real influence in some states, is better understood in the aggregate as *nominal*.

Conclusion

What do the Johnson, Reagan, and Bush cases say about the conditions under which the public can achieve real policy influence? The best chance comes when a just-elected president concludes that he cannot succeed in Congress without mounting a new campaign for public support. Lyndon Johnson, who did not need any postelection help, did not seek it. The smothering mandate assumption sparked by his landslide election effectively removed voters from the game, eliminating their opportunity for any real influence over the shape of legislation. Divided government and weak electoral credentials, however, forced both Reagan and Bush to ask for help. The Reagan case effectively defines what real voter policy influence in such circumstances can achieve, and shows that when a public decides to support the agenda it can enter into a partnership with the president.

Why was the public more influential in the Reagan than in the Bush case? Bush, after all, was by far the weakest of these three presidents and the most in need of public help. In this case, the public had perhaps its greatest opportunity to help shape the terms of a partnership and the content of the policy, or, failing that, to kill it outright for lack of support. But majority opinion, though both clear and consistent in the Reagan case, was neither in the early months of the Bush administration. The Bush case suggests that the surest way for voters to lose their chance for real influence is to express ambivalence. It is doubtful, for example, that a politically weak new president like Bush could have overcome a public if it were as united in opposition to his plan as the public that united in support of Reagan's. The confused state of the public opinion that Bush faced gave him the opening he needed to sell his election victory as the only clear and legitimate expression of the will of the people. And it reduced the perceived political risk to congressional Democrats tempted to support his tax cut. Even a weak president might prevail if opinion is mixed and indifferent enough to be dismissed.

We can conclude that the key to real voter policy influence is the combination of presidential weakness and public unity. Future presidential weakness — in the form of divided government and/or narrow victory margins — seems highly likely. Thus it is easy to predict that new influence opportunities for voters will arise. But future voter unity, though probable, is harder to forecast confidently, given its usual dependence on problems and crises. Those who would encourage that presidents and the public come to terms on major policy choices before legislation passes will ask what can be done besides passively awaiting the coincidence of presidential weakness and crisis-inspired public unity. They should start by asking how voter unity can be achieved in the absence of crisis. That raises questions of motivation and incentives, the next subject before us.

Chapter 5
Policy Partnerships:
What Would It Take?

The key function of elections in democratic theory is to ensure the responsiveness of public officials to the preferences of citizens. That elevates voter policy influence to the top of democracy's hierarchy of values, securely above such recently prominent concerns as social capital (e.g., Putnam 2000) and deliberation (e.g., Fishkin 1995). The problem, as we have seen, is that, in contemporary American political practice, such influence is not only weak but also in decline. The decline is documented by the research cited in Chapter 1, and the weakness is apparent in the analyses of the workings of direct, anticipatory, and legitimizing influence contained in Chapters 2, 3, and 4, respectively.

Anticipatory influence, described earlier as the "bedrock of voter influence," ensures that any candidate for high office, including a president who hopes to be reelected, will think carefully about potential electoral consequences before speaking or acting on major policy questions. This is unquestionably a necessary and important source of voter influence, but, by the standards that have been suggested, it is not sufficient. The reasons include the imperfections noted in Chapter 3 (most notably delayed, blurred, and/or evaded accountability). The most important shortcoming is that exclusive reliance on anticipation leaves pre-enactment citizen influence entirely out of account.

I do not believe that voters should dictate all policy, but I do believe (as stated in the Preface) that they should have more opportunity than they now have to come to terms with presidents, at least on the big questions, before policy is enacted. "Big questions" implies questions that most directly concern the largest number of people — questions that matter because they touch so many lives, such as the future of Social Security and of health care.

Means: Supplement Anticipatory Influence

What, then, can effectively supplement anticipatory influence? Short of impractical changes in the constitutional rules (such as empowering citizens to set national policy via binding referenda — see Cronin 1989), we are forced back to direct and legitimizing influence. Both are, after all, about presidents and voters coming to terms before policy is enacted, and both also address delayed and blurred accountability problems by directing attention to expected results of vital importance to the mass public.

In theory, this can encourage disciplined retrospective voting that holds presidents to strict account. In practice, however, neither direct nor legitimizing influence comes into play often enough or forcefully enough to keep the electorate focused on expected results. Without a compelling reason to stay focused on a specific policy, few people will even notice which among many campaign promises a president tries to keep.

What if these two forms of pre-enactment influence could somehow be cobbled together and made more prominent features of electoral politics? What if this happened by design rather than by happenstance? And what if both were simultaneously brought to bear on a single issue known to be of great importance to voters? If all this came to pass, two good things would happen.

First, voters would by definition be more intensely engaged as policy is debated and set. They would therefore be much more likely to see themselves as cocreators of the policy. Second, such engagement would also very probably sharpen the focus of mass attention on specific expected results, thus increasing the likelihood that politicians would be held to strict account for those results. The upshot would be a net increase in the quality, if not necessarily the quantity, of voter policy influence.

That, in any case, is the future that is projected and elaborated here. Such an ordered combination of voter-friendly circumstances is well within the realm of possibility, and this and the concluding chapter will show how it might be brought about.

There is much to elaborate and more than a few questions to consider; all will be addressed in due course. The essential proposal can be stated simply, however: use voter pressure (direct influence) to get presidential candidates to agree to push for specific legislation approved in advance by voters. That legitimizes the policy proposal (legitimizing influence) and visibly puts the candidate and the people in business together (policy partnership). Such a high-profile partnership gives the newly elected president a real (as opposed to an unverified) mandate. That, in turn, increases the likelihood that Congress will actually pass the legislation.

The Problem: Presidents Will Not Partner

There is need for a plan like this because although mandate claims are common (and generally meaningless; see Dahl 1990), real partnerships that produce real mandates are extremely rare.

Most presidents simply leave the public out of their legislative strategies altogether. As we saw in Chapter 4, just three of the ten men to hold the office since 1956 made serious efforts as candidates and/or new presidents to implicate the public in their policy designs. And of that three, only Republican president Ronald Reagan in 1980 had to show *real* public support, after the election, to get his tax and budget cuts through a resistant Democratic House of Representatives. If he hadn't repeatedly demonstrated strong majority support for his tax and budget cuts during his postelection campaign for the bills, they would not have passed. Voters thus held the trump card. They could just as easily have killed the legislation as ensured its passage. That is what made their influence real.

The other two, Lyndon Johnson and George W. Bush, both claimed the voter seal of approval for their signature education and tax-cut bills without actually demonstrating it. Both claims were credited by enough members of Congress to help the legislation to pass. The poll evidence reviewed in Chapter 4 shows more public indifference in the Johnson case, and ambivalence in the Bush case, however, than anything like enthusiastic voter endorsement in either case. In effect, the voter seal of approval was presumed and exploited while the true state of public opinion was ignored.

The lesson most likely to be drawn by candidates and presidents from the examples of Johnson and Bush is that it is possible to get credit for public support without actually demonstrating it. Why, then, should any such figure bother with real partnerships if legislation can be passed just by claiming support? Presidents rarely see any reasons, but we see three.

The first reason is long-term self-interest. Most presidents want more than just a victory on a single legislative vote. They want to build a majority party, and cultivating a partnership on high-priority legislation can be a good first step toward that goal. Voters are more likely to develop loyalty to an agenda that they help to set and pass.

The second reason is that it can help the political system overcome ideological gridlock. For example, a partnership strategy can be used to end the longstanding impasse between market versus government solutions to problems of health care and Social Security by structuring an election season to help force a choice.

The third reason is because it is the right thing to do. It is democratically reasonable to expect presidents to occasionally risk implicating voters in the policy process as real partners. In other words, let them say "yea" or "nay," as in the Reagan case. Historically, the public has greatly empowered the presidency; let presidents reciprocate by empowering the people from time to time.

If we really want presidents to do this, however, the record shows that we will have to make them. The question is whether that is possible.

The Solution: Pressure

I think that it is. The reason is that something like this has been done before. Consider the example of Ross Perot in 1992.

The Perot case shows that it is not impossible for an outside force to intervene and change the dynamic of a presidential election by magnifying the importance of public opinion to the policy debate. Before Perot proved otherwise, many would have scoffed at the idea that any outsider could shape the policy debate like he did in 1992. To be sure, other third-party candidates such as Theodore Roosevelt in 1912 and Ralph Nader in 2000 have influenced election outcomes, but none has used Perot's methods or matched his impact on the policy debate.[1]

Perot had his quirks and faults, but what matters here is that he achieved three things that can usefully be made to happen again. (1) He mounted a series of policy briefings that constituted a national tutorial on an important problem (the federal budget deficit); (2) he persuaded even more of the electorate than the sizable number that already did so to assign a high priority to that problem, and (3) he forced the mainstream candidates to respond by addressing the problem much more frequently and forthrightly than they otherwise would have done (Buchanan 1995). In the end, the election handed new president, Bill Clinton, a "fix the deficit" mandate that, somewhat against his will, he acted on in his first budget. He later received significant credit for addressing the deficit, which he was glad to accept.

These are just the kinds of outcomes that the new agents and actions proposed here are intended to achieve.

Admittedly, Perot had unique assets that greatly magnified his impact: novelty marquee value, unlimited money, unprecedented access to free media, and an audience made responsive by disenchantment with the mainstream candidates. He also had significant liabilities, however, most notably the temperamental quirks that eventually destroyed his credibility. What this suggests is that similar outcomes can be achieved by an *institution* that makes use of interesting personalities without being undermined by them.

The first and most important step, then, is to establish such an institution. I therefore propose the creation of something to be called the *American Citizens' Foundation*.[2]

The American Citizens' Foundation

Why create a new institution? Why not simply ask existing institutions, such as the two major political parties, to work toward these worthy outcomes? Because parties, like the candidates and special interests that they serve, are not interested in increasing voter policy influence. They want voters to empower them, not vice versa. In the effort to win elective offices, which is their legitimate *raison d'être*, parties often find it necessary to give priority to narrower electoral, ideological, and economic interests that can and often do conflict with aggregate voter preferences. Like the candidates described in Chapter 2, parties give top priority to aggregate voter preferences only when failure to do so lowers the chance for victory at the polls. Because only crises are powerful enough to mobilize such spontaneous voter demand, and because such crises are relatively rare, we need institutional help to facilitate the coordination of voter demand in the noncrisis electoral circumstances that are far more common. The premise, again, is that on matters of particular importance to them, voters should have a voice even when they are not spontaneously moved to collective action by widespread alarm.

Voters therefore need a new institution to serve their interests in noncrisis election seasons because, at present, the only voices broadcast widely enough to dominate the airwaves during presidential election seasons usually speak for narrower partisan, ideological, or economic interests. Missing is a nonpartisan, noncommercial voice, backed by the resources needed to reach and engage the American people as a whole in a sustained dialogue about their common stakes as they approach the choice of a president. Those common stakes will sometimes feature policy questions with partnership potential.

Objectives

The purpose of the American Citizens' Foundation (ACF), then, is to give the voting public, whose clear preferences are underrepresented in many controversial policy debates, better access to its own electoral leverage so that it can exert more influence on candidate issue priorities and stands as well as on the prospects for legislative action.

The foundation will not try to displace or supplant the familiar partisan fight for votes, but it will try to increase candidate responsiveness to the policy preferences of the electorate. Here is how it will work.

Basic Strategy The idea is to introduce the policy partnership concept only in carefully chosen election years when it makes sense to do so. (See the later discussion of strategic choices.) In such years, the ACF will ask the best experts to develop the fairest possible descriptions of a single national problem that voters identify as among the most important facing the country. The same experts will then be asked to generate realistic partisan options for solving the top problem — model proposals that reflect the most influential Republican and Democratic policy thinking and that are suitable for endorsement by the major party candidates.

Thereafter, the foundation will extensively publicize the fruits of this policy analysis via paid advertising. Finally, it will use sophisticated polling to ensure a steady supply of information, also widely publicized, about how mass opinion is evolving.

In theory, the policy advertising will strengthen the voter policy consensus, which will put added pressure on the candidates to respond by embracing the model party options. The practical test will be whether ACF briefings and polls and postelection voter lobbying (discussed below) help to sufficiently enhance the credibility and import of public opinion to get newly elected presidents to act on their promises to actually submit legislation and work to get the Congress to enact it. While voters can achieve significantly increased levels of influence, short of helping to define the content of policy, legislation that can be attributed to voter influence (as enhanced by ACF programs) is the ultimate indicator of impact and success, for both voters and the ACF.[3]

Five Required Capabilities If the candidates respond, leverage has been exerted. To see that candidates do respond, the AFC needs five specific capabilities.

1. Inform and strengthen the existing voter consensus The first is the ability to inform and strengthen the voter consensus in support of action on a national problem. As already noted, the ACF would not move unless there is a pre-existing voter consensus. In fact, there often is. As Table 1.1 showed, majority agreement on the identity of the top election-season policy problem emerged in four of the thirteen elections between 1956 and 2000, and there were pluralities above 40 percent in three additional elections. The credibility of the partnership strategy depends on majority or large plurality numbers like these, because such are needed to plausibly claim to represent the "will of the people" and not just an aggregation of partisan or special-interest blocs. Foundation polling will establish the extent of cross-partisan unity and other demographic patterns within percentages expressing support for the target problem and disclose the information.

The fact that more than half of the elections in Table 1.1 featured a public sufficiently unified to "partner" if offered the chance is normatively important because voters and not ACF staffers or contractors should set the agenda. It is also pragmatically necessary because getting voters to buy into new priorities is prohibitively difficult. Research shows, for example, that presidents find it harder than usually imagined to build public support for their policy initiatives (Edwards 2003). The people, it seems, will not respond to a presidential call for policy support unless they already attach a high priority to the problem the policy addresses. By this reasoning, Ronald Reagan could not have moved the public to endorse his then-radical tax-cut proposal had not some 60 percent of those eligible to vote already concluded that the economy needed top-priority attention. Although they were skeptical about his plan before they chose him as president, once he was elected the people were inclined to respond to his request that they help him persuade Congress pass the legislation.

A good reason to believe that the ACF can use expert policy analysis and advertising to inform and strengthen a pre-existing voter consensus is because, as noted, it has been done before. Consider the impact that Ross Perot had in 1992 on the public awareness of the federal budget deficit and its perceived importance to the nation. Perot produced eleven thirty-minute commercials, fifteen sixty-second commercials, and five thirty-second commercials, many detailing the budget deficit problem (Barta 1993, 329). This educational effort, which attracted large audiences, had a measurable impact on the importance the public attached to the budget-deficit problem. Polls conducted by Princeton Survey Research Associates before and after Perot's reentry into the race on October 1, 1992, showed a thirteen-point increase (from 18 to 31) in the percentage of voters identifying the budget deficit as the most important problem facing the nation. This was the single largest increase for any issue during the campaign. Only Perot's consistent hammering of the need to reduce the deficit can explain such a jump (Buchanan, 1995). Expertly managed, an ACF education and advertising effort can aspire to a similar impact.

2. Increase the political significance of public opinion Once the maximum consensus has been achieved, the most important thing that the ACF can do to enhance voter influence is to increase the political significance of public opinion. How? With extensive and regular polling that comes to define the public will on the target problem. There is nothing like this now; instead, there is only the occasional (and irregular) poll asking voters to rank "the most important problems facing the country." With the ACF, there will be weekly policy priority polling, advertised to make it a prominent feature of the ongoing presidential campaign. The aim is to attach political costs to ignoring the public's preferences and to make it impossible for candidates to ignore or downplay or misrepresent the true state of public opinion, as Lyndon Johnson and George W. Bush did.

Why is such a practice not already commonplace? One reason is the palpable lack of respect among political practitioners and scholars for the often uninformed state of public opinion. Another is widespread skepticism about the reliability and validity of typical poll measures, given the vagaries of sampling and the wording of questions, plus the fact that most polls are but one-time snapshots of ever-changing sentiment. Both kinds of reservations severely limit the credibility of polls as actionable influences on the setting of national policy.[4]

Patricia Conley's 2001 study of presidential mandates provides a convenient illustration of how decisively these reservations have marginalized direct measures of public opinion. She argues that although voter preferences matter, they matter only as they are inferred and interpreted by elites. One reason, she says, is the evidence that "a large proportion of voters is ignorant of the issues and cannot accurately identify the candidates' platforms" (2001, 4). That is why, in her effort to predict mandates, she thought it more sensible to examine what mandate rhetoric means to politicians than to "establish whether the public is sufficiently informed to justify a presidential mandate claim" (2001, 6). She notes that poll results also do not figure very prominently in the calculations of politicians. She points up the ambiguity and unreliability of poll data and concludes:

> The best way for politicians to forecast the future (i.e., to estimate how an issue's fate in the election may translate into a prediction of its' fate in the legislature) is to examine multiple sources of data (e.g., "national, state and local election tabulations; national, state, and local polls reported in the press; and news accounts of national, state, and local political conditions") when testing their hypotheses and *to rely on behavior such as votes, rather than poll results.* (2001, 37; emphasis added)

Another reason why poll evidence is downplayed is that politicians like the freedom to maneuver, which they have when public expectations are ambiguous. This occurs when expectations are incoherent, or when they can be portrayed as such. In fact, the electorate typically is passive and ill informed, which usually does leave politicians free to interpret the will of the people in ways described by Conley. She claims that, despite all this, there are "incentives for accuracy" in interpretation, which is undoubtedly true. But the point to notice here is that the interpretive process is largely an "insider's game" in which elites decide what the current evidence of public opinion means, and therefore elites feel free to credit a consent claim like Lyndon Johnson's or George W. Bush's despite the existence of unsupportive evidence.

This is exactly the practice that the ACF would penetrate and disrupt. The way to do so is suggested by the fact that, under certain circumstances, poll-tested public opinion is very likely to get a respectful hearing from politicians. When there are clear, unambiguous, majority, or significant-plurality public expectations that endure across time, and when those expectations are thought to have electoral consequences, politicians will attend to them even if such expectations are made apparent largely through polling data (Buchanan 2004, 96–105).

3. Press candidates to endorse the model partisan solutions Authoritative public opinion creates the leverage needed to achieve the third necessary foundation capability, which is to put intense pressure on the candidates to endorse the model partisan solutions. This is done by including in the advertising a call for candidates to pledge to seek passage of their partisan model. This is similar to the "no new taxes" pledge extracted from Republican candidates at all levels by Grover Norquist, president of the conservative group, Americans for Tax Reform (ATR). The "pledge" tactic has been very effective for ATR and it can be similarly effective for the ACF.

The partisan legitimacy of the model stances depends of the inclusion of highly respected partisan experts at the ACF problem-definition and policy-analysis stages. That practice increases the likelihood of bipartisan agreement on the problem definition (which does exist, for example, on Social Security and health care) and within-party agreement on the principle solutions most likely to be acceptable to each party's eventual nominee (see the health-care scenario in Chapter 6). An example of this kind of policy briefing was a bipartisan conference hosted in the spring of 2003 by the Lyndon Baines Johnson Presidential Library and the Lyndon B. Johnson School of Public Affairs at the University of Texas on the major options for improving the national health-care system (Big Choices, 2003).

Once legitimate partisan models have been made available and publicized, the task becomes bringing public pressure to bear to get the candidates to endorse them. A relevant example is again supplied by Ross Perot. Following his well-publicized explanation of the budget deficit problem, Perot mounted a second public-relations campaign to force candidates George H.W. Bush and Bill Clinton to address the issue in 1992. The campaign included television advertising and op-ed columns demanding that the candidates offer concrete plans, plus the announcement and advertisement of his own model plan for reducing the deficit. The promise of the scheme was suggested by a front-page *Wall Street Journal* story: "With his strong emphasis on the need to reduce the federal deficit Mr. Perot may well increase the pressure on the other two candidates to address the issue in a more specific way" (Shribman and Noah, 1992, A1). What Perot was doing, of course, was ratcheting up the public pressure, as private polling conducted by Bush and Clinton clearly showed. Such leverage did eventually force the two men to pay much more attention to the deficit than they otherwise would have.

Some of Perot's methods, such as paid ads exhorting the candidates to address the consensus, can easily be adopted by the ACF. Others are less perfect fits, however, and require adjustment. For example, Perot, who withdrew and then returned to the 1992 race as a candidate, issued his own detailed proposal. The ACF, which endorses no candidate or proposal until after the voters have spoken (see the discussion of the fifth required capability, below) will instead publicize the model Democratic and Republican plans developed during its issue-study phase and will then publicly challenge the candidates during the fall campaign to embrace them or justify a refusal to do so.

What happens if ACF and other polls show a clear voter preference for one model partisan plan over another during the course of the campaign?

The disadvantaged candidate would be expected to do what all office seekers in such circumstances do: tailor a proposal to increase its attractiveness (see the vignette at the end of this chapter). The concern of the ACF is only to ensure that any modification a candidate makes to a model partisan plan remains a realistic approach to solving the problem and is straightforward about the costs and who will bear them.

This proved to be an issue in the case of Perot and the deficit. The Texas billionaire did get the major party candidates to pay more attention to the deficit, but he did not succeed in forcing them to present truly serious deficit-reduction plans (Murray 1992, A1). That outcome suggests that his leverage techniques were, from the ACF perspective, insufficient. To them can be added additional weaponry from the standard bag of campaign tricks. The ACF will retain the services of the best available political consultants to devise attack ads and other pressure tactics aimed at forcing reluctant candidates to offer detailed plans.

4. Keep the issue on the front burner during the campaign Once the size and intensity of pre-existing public agreement on the top-priority problem has reached its potential, and assuming that the candidates have put forward acceptable plans, the problem becomes keeping the issue on the front burner during the campaign. Candidates, who are issue-opportunists, will experiment with a variety of topics in search of a competitive edge. The ACF cannot prevent that, but it can put intense pressure on the major candidates to keep the target issue in reasonable focus throughout the campaign. The pressure can involve both carrots (e.g., free TV time to debate or present on the issue) and sticks (attack ads and other efforts to stigmatize any candidate who ignores the top-policy debate for too long). The key point here is that the pressure must be sustained, particularly during the two-month period from Labor Day to Election Day.

This is an extraordinarily challenging task, because campaigns are famous for surprise twists and turns that can change the subject forever in an instant. Consider just a few examples. Within a month of his 1841 inauguration as president, William Henry Harrison died, radically altering the postelection policy agenda (Crockett 2002, 62). In 1956, foreign policy crises erupted just weeks before Election Day, fundamentally changing the issue priorities of candidates Dwight D. Eisenhower and Adlai Stevenson and the voters trying to decide between them. And in 1976 and 2000, debate performances by Gerald Ford and Al Gore, respectively, switched the stakes from issues to candidate strengths and weaknesses for many voters overnight.

The effort to keep the discussion focused on the top issue cannot be immune to such unforeseen circumstances, but respected capabilities in policy analysis, polling, and advertising will help the ACF to remain a force to be reckoned with. The fallback position is to use the pledge (if the winner took it) to revive the issue after the election.

5. Mobilize voters to contact Congress The fifth and final ACF task (and necessary capability) is to help the new president mobilize public support to win congressional approval for his solution to the top-policy problem. The main technique here is a massive "contact your congressperson and senator" drive, again fueled by ACF advertising. Congress is particularly sensitive to direct citizen lobbying, which makes this lobbying potentially very effective. Such citizen proactivity also has special symbolic and practical importance to the ACF mission, however, because any citizen who takes the trouble to personally contact a member of Congress by that action turns a theoretical ideal — the policy partnership — into a concrete reality. He or she does so by making a conscious decision to go into business with the president in the effort to get legislation enacted, thus assuming the status of a player with a stake in the outcome. This is the *ne plus ultra* of the policy partnership.

A citizen mobilization, however, can be expected to happen only in certain circumstances. The president must want the help, and he must satisfy two conditions. First is that he win the largest share of the popular vote (George W. Bush, who lost the popular vote in 2000, would not have qualified), and second is that the election can be shown by ACF polling to have "mandated" the new president's proposed solution to the top-policy problem. That is, the poll data must show that a majority of those who gave the president the largest vote share intended the vote to be an explicit endorsement not just of the candidate, and not just of the preeminence of the problem, but also of the president-elect's specific proposal for solving the problem. (For an example of a polling procedure that can pinpoint such information, see Buchanan 2004, 81–94). Under this provision, Reagan, whose policy support at his 1980 election was mixed, would not have qualified.

The rationale for these conditions is simple. The ACF cannot act unless the people have signaled their support. For ACF purposes, majority rule trumps the Electoral College, and documented mandates trump elite bargains. These are deliberately stringent rules, because a nonpartisan foundation whose avowed constituency is the American electorate has no business endorsing anything without an authoritative mandate from that source. The partnership potential remains alive, however, because any future new president who failed to meet either test can still mount an independent campaign for a postelection mandate, as both Reagan and the younger Bush chose to do.

Finally, this question: why would a president who can pass the "majority vote" and "mandate" tests need any outside help to get legislation through Congress? Because there is never any guarantee that Congress will honor an electoral mandate without additional prodding. A controversial issue with a history of congressional deadlock, which describes the education issue in 1964 or health care at the time of this writing, poses a significant legislative challenge for any president under any political circumstances. To prevail on the Elementary and Secondary Education Act of 1965, for example, Lyndon Johnson, who won the 1964 election by a landslide (Table 4.1), had to engage in extensive maneuvering and lobbying in Congress. A future president in a similar position might welcome a supplemental "outside game" provided in part by the ACF.

The closely divided state of American politics suggests that future opportunities for the ACF to offer postelection help are at best unpredictable. It is important to remember, however, that just getting a problem on the policy agenda — one that would otherwise not be there, as happens in the scenario set out later in this chapter — is a significant display of public influence.

Strategic Choices

Next come three choices aimed at giving the work of the ACF a disciplined focus. The first is that the ACF will be active only during election seasons. The second and third require that the ACF decide what the right questions and circumstances are, respectively. Let us consider each in turn.

Election Seasons Only Presidents may "go public" at any time in search of help in Congress. Why not consider deploying the ACF whenever a president wants help? In part because, as just noted, the president's electoral performance determines eligibility for ACF help, but also because election seasons — by which I mean campaigns, elections, and their immediate aftermaths — provide the best opportunities for presidents and citizens to come to terms on policy.

Election seasons attract maximum public attention. During this brief window, millions of citizens are inspired, in ways not otherwise true, to concern themselves with national politics and policy. They are more willing to learn, potentially more open to influence, and generally more willing to take some part in the national political community than they are at other times. In short, election seasons offer the best natural, regularly scheduled forum for serious national conversations about prospective policy.

Also during election seasons, large cash reserves often permit candidates to promote policy agendas extensively, showcasing one or more proposals intended as the signature legislative initiatives in the presidency to follow. This permits the ACF to leverage its investment, to the extent that it can encourage candidates to use their resources to promote the target issue.

The most important reason for the ACF to be active only during election seasons, however, is that there is no better regularly scheduled opportunity for maximum popular influence than an election season. Legislative success never matters more to a president than it does right after the first election. That is when the president's policy-making prowess is most on trial. As Richard Neustadt argues, it is any president's *first* battles that decide the public image and create a pattern for a Washington reputation (1990, 143). Precisely because he is on trial, popular support for the agenda will never be more welcome. Important public influence opportunities do sometimes arise outside of election seasons, but they are less predictable and usually less consequential.

The Right Questions An outside agency like ACF should not try to turn every question, not even every important question, into a partnership target. Certain guidelines for choice suggest themselves. For example, minor issues, such as whether daylight savings time should be standardized nationally, are obviously not good candidates. Questions that polarize intense minorities, like those dealing with abortion, gay rights, flag burning, stem-cell research, or affirmative action, are probably best left to the temporizations of politicians and the decompression afforded by the judicial process. And some portentous decisions — like the Spring, 2003 debate over whether or not to initiate a war with Iraq — emerge and are thus necessarily settled outside the electoral context and can reflect public opinion only when the president takes into account anticipated public reaction at the next election before deciding.

Problems that are already widely perceived to require urgent attention do not need any outside promotion. They are likely to feature spontaneous voter-driven agenda setting, as with the 1960 public demand that the new president meet the Soviet threat or the 1992 demand that the winner address economic problems including the deficit.

The best potential partnership questions involve nationally important long-term problems not yet perceived to be in full crisis mode but that can benefit from and thus ideally should receive timely debate to clarify options and choices.

For example, how best to reform an entitlement program like Social Security is a good partnership question. So, too, is the question of when and how to undertake infrastructure upgrades like the interstate highway system built during the Eisenhower administration. Other promising classes of questions include those long stalemated by partisan wrangling, such as the budget-deficit deadlock that existed between 1982 and 1990, or ideological debates that cannot be resolved by empirical proof, such as those over the comparative merits of tax cuts versus deficit reduction as the best way to stimulate a sluggish economy. A particularly good candidate, the focus of Chapter 6, is the issue of health-care access and affordability, notably for those who are not covered by Medicare or Medicaid. This issue has been mired in ideological fights over market versus regulatory solutions to cost and accessibility problems, which have frozen the policy debate for decades. A partnership strategy can unfreeze that debate by clarifying the options and legitimizing a policy choice.

The Right Circumstances The ACF will mount a policy partnership campaign only during election seasons, but it will not do so in every such season. It will instead pick its spots, moving only when the time is right. In nonpartnership election years, the foundation will engage in limited civic education, sponsored research, and get-out-the-vote efforts, as described in the original Markle Commission proposal (see Note 2 and Buchanan 1991, 157); it will continuing its fund-raising and issue-analysis activities in preparation for partnership years (see the upcoming discussion of operations).

At issue is when will an external push be maximally useful. Most promising are election seasons that feature significant long-term problems already recognized as high priorities by voter pluralities but that are in danger of being ignored by candidates wishing to avoid political costs or to emphasize what they regard as politically more advantageous issues. For example, Table 1.1 showed that in 1976, 1988, and 1996 significant pluralities called for action on economic problems that never did receive center-stage attention from the candidates. Outside pressure might have led some of those candidates, whose electoral calculations led them to sidestep or downplay economic issues, to choose otherwise.

Other election years shown in Table 1.1 would have been harder calls, because they featured fewer inviting circumstances. The budget deficit was prominent, for example, in 1984, and was ignored as an issue by the sure winner, incumbent president Ronald Reagan. But the public's highest-priority problem, identified by a plurality of just 30 percent, involved international affairs, with economic concerns in second place at 22 percent (not depicted in Table 1.1). The fact that there *was* a sure winner — a popular incumbent president firmly opposed to addressing the deficit — was a daunting barrier to initiating a conversation about it. That would have made getting it high on the campaign agenda just as difficult for an outside agency like the ACF as it proved to be for Reagan's 1984 opponent, former vice president Walter Mondale.

A year in which an incumbent is seeking reelection will generally be a poor time to jump in, if only because it is so difficult to make the election about anything other than the first-term performance. An early July 2003 *CBS News* poll, for example, showed that a plurality of 39 percent identified the economy and jobs as the most important problem facing the country, followed by "War/Iraq/Foreign policy" and "Terrorism (general)" in second and third place, at 10 and 9 percent, respectively. Thus the 2004 Democratic Party presidential candidates were busy testing criticisms of the sluggish economy and the president's exaggerations of the Iraqi threat and mismanagement of the reconstruction effort in Iraq in their effort to undercut the still-popular Bush's strongest claim to reelection: his post–September 11 management of national security. An earlier (spring 2003) effort by the Democrats to bring up the health-care issue had little impact, as the July *CBS News* poll showed just 4 percent considered it the most important problem (PollingReport.com/priorities). That did not mean that health care was of no concern to Americans. In an August 2003 Pew Research Center poll, for example, 67 percent of a large national sample favored having the government guarantee health care for all citizens even if it meant repealing the Bush tax cuts or raising taxes! It did suggest, however, that the health-care issue might be too easily submerged by events touching the higher priorities to warrant an ACF investment in the issue. In the same Pew poll, for example, 57 percent said the president should be focused on the economy, and 27 percent on the war on terrorism (*http://people-press.org/reports/pdf/190.pdf*). Clearly, too many crosscurrents were already in play.

A selective approach to issues and circumstances means that partnerships may happen only somewhat more frequently under this proposal than they would have happened on their own; perhaps once in ten or fifteen rather than once in fifty years. (In the fictional scenarios set out later, I posit that the first two will come in rapid succession — also a possibility.)

Whatever the frequency turns out to be, even a single respectable demonstration can have beneficial spillover effects. Much like the unprecedented use of attack advertising in the1988 presidential campaign heightened sensitivity to attack strategies in subsequent elections, a meaningful ACF intervention on behalf of a top voter priority will raise the subsequent profile of voter priorities. How candidates treat those priorities when the ACF is not in the game will be widely noticed. Candidates, hoping to head off another intervention, may take pains to prove them unnecessary. In this way, the threat and the occasional fact of additional interventions can result in a net increase in public influence.

Foundation Operations

This is not the place for detailed budgets, blueprints, or action plans, but I do want to say something about the resources and organizational capabilities needed to implement what has been proposed. The following discussion will touch briefly on the operational side of the ACF. As it suggests, such a venture, while doable, is neither inexpensive nor simple.

Finance The ACF will have relatively modest annual expenses associated with staffing and supporting a small permanent organization of approximately fifteen people, and occasional bursts of greatly increased spending associated with policy partnership campaigns. The latter expenses include contracting for and supervising the specialized polling, consulting, and advertising services described earlier in this chapter, and defraying the costs of television advertising and other programming.

In intervention years, expenditures will be comparable to the polling and advertising costs of a presidential campaign, but the range of potential costs is better approximated by using comparisons to recent third-party campaigns than to major-party-candidate spending. One obvious spending benchmark is the 1992 Perot campaign. Between February and December of that year, Perot spent $69 million (Barta 1993, xvii). The bulk of this was for television time, as would also be the case for ACF. Perot also had expenses the ACF will not incur, however, such as financing his effort to get on the ballot in all fifty states.

Another useful comparison is supplied by third-party candidate Pat Buchanan, who spent just over $39 million in the 2000 presidential election (opensecrets.org). Also relevant is the amount spent to defeat the Clinton health-care proposal in 1993; according to one estimate, the medical, insurance, and small-business lobbies spent $50 million in an advertising, public-relations, and lobbying campaign (Shapiro 2003, 31).

Taking into account that ACF expenditures on television time can vary dramatically with the dynamic of a campaign, an initial estimate of the potential range of "typical" ACF single-season total spending in a partnership year, in 2003 dollars, is between $40 and $60 million, including organizational startup and operating costs. By comparison, 2000 major party candidates George W. Bush and Al Gore spent $186 million and $120 million, respectively.

Where will the money come from? The foundation will seek the resources it needs from five sources: (1) a consortium of existing foundations, whose voluntary contributions will count under a law requiring foundations to devote 5 percent of their assets annually to the support of charities; (2) the federal government, by a tax-form check-off like that supporting campaign finance; (3) a program of citizen solicitation, via the Internet, and also promoted as a regular feature of the program and policy advertising described earlier; (4) specially targeted grant seeking and fundraising; and (5) returns on endowment investments.

Structure The ACF is to be both an "operating" foundation (i.e., it will run some of its own programs and services) and a "granting" foundation (i.e., it will contract out, via a series of time-bound grants to third parties that have the specialized skills needed to provide the necessary services). (See Strom 2003, A1.)

Mission Control The programs and services that the ACF will staff and run out of its permanent organization are those associated with amassing an endowment and building the bipartisan credibility needed to win the attention of the news media, the loyalty and support of the voters, and the respect of presidential candidates.

The imprimatur of the foundation is to be exercised by a blue-ribbon advisory body, a board of trustees, made up of both Republicans and Democrats whose stature enhances the credibility of the ACF and its work. Examples include former elected officials (such as former presidents and senators), intellectuals, educators, news media executives, journalists, philanthropists, and citizens. The board exists to ensure that the enterprise stays true to its long-term aim of strengthening American democracy. It is also responsible for staffing and supervising the permanent organization.

Once in place, the organization and its staff are responsible for long-term planning for programs, recommending policy interventions to the board, supervising contract services, and developing the endowment.

Permanent employees will include a foundation president and several programs and grants officers, institutional fundraisers, and endowment managers.

Contract Services Contract services will include policy analysis, polling, focus group and other forms of public opinion assessment, plus television advertising and political-consulting services. The issue-analysis is to be done by recognized experts taking partisan ideas and arguments into account. The polling is to be done by major contracting firms — such as Gallup, Harris, Pew, and Princeton Survey Research Associates, among others — according to the polling objectives described earlier.

The Future of Public Influence

It remains to see how this plan might actually work in practice. We close this chapter, therefore, with a brief fictional sketch, cast as journalism, in which the new machinery is used to get hypothetical candidates to offer and debate long-term solutions to a problem they would have preferred to ignore: Social Security reform. The vignette also serves to introduce the subject of the final chapter: health care.

PUBLIC INTEREST GROUP, IN NEW BID TO ENLIST VOTERS, TRUMPETS HEALTH-CARE ISSUE

Dateline — Washington, D.C., August 15, 2011

The nonpartisan American Citizen's Foundation announced today that its blue-ribbon advisory panel has selected health-care reform as a "policy partnership" issue for the upcoming presidential election.

This is the second time that the foundation, established in 2005, has chosen to enter the fray in hopes of influencing the policy debate.

The advisory team — a group of former elected officials, journalists, academic policy experts, and citizens — argued in its report that the nation's long-standing inability to slow the rise in heath-care costs and the increase in the number of citizens without health insurance justified another effort to make the presidential campaign a referendum on an unsolved public-policy problem. The hope is that the candidates will propose clear solutions so that expected voter endorsement of the election winner's proposal will encourage timely legislative action.

The foundation, commonly referred to as the ACF, helped to spark a 2008 campaign debate on Social Security, which observers credited with assisting the eventual passage of the Social Security Reform Act of 2009. Spokesperson and former senator Olympia Snowe (R-Maine) said that a well-timed and well-crafted advertising campaign, plus innovative polling techniques, helped to crystallize public opinion around the issue.

Candidates and campaign officials at first took little note of the initiative, but attention picked up after a series of polls showed increasing public reaction to a barrage of infomercials and television advertisements put up by the ACF in early September. The presentations explained the Social Security problem and offered "model" Democratic and Republican options for solving it that had been developed at a series of bipartisan policy briefings sponsored by the group late in 2007.

Each model plan offered a menu of tough fund-raising measures capable of restoring the fiscal health of the retirement system. The Democrats called for making income levels above the current cut-off of $87,000 subject to Social Security taxes, and a 2 percent increase in the capital gains tax, with the revenues earmarked for rebuilding a Social Security trust fund surplus. The Republican plan raised the Social Security tax rate paid by workers and employers to 7.16 from 6.2 percent, established optional private investment accounts that permitted workers to invest up to two percentage points of the 7.16 percent payroll tax. The setup cost of the private accounts was to be financed by means-testing eligibility for benefits. Means-testing meant that only low-to-moderate income earners would be eligible for full Social Security benefits.

Although the model plans were shaped by policy experts ideologically committed to their respective parties, the proposals were much more detailed and candid about costs and who would pay them than candidate proposals usually are during election campaigns. The issue-promotion group believes that asking candidates to endorse plans vetted by partisan experts that voters have already seen in ACF advertising will give candidates enough political cover to risk endorsing realistic solutions during the campaign

The 2008 hopefuls were caught off guard when mid-September polls showed that voters wanted candidates to spell out what they would do to head off a problem still decades away from crisis. The most recent Social Security system trustees report showed that tax revenues were not expected to fall below benefit expenses until 2018, and that the Social Security trust fund would not be exhausted until 2042.

Each candidate initially took refuge in standard partisan rhetoric. Former Vermont governor Howard Dean, the Democratic nominee, swore to protect the existing Social Security system from Republican efforts to cut payments to future retirees in order to finance a risky "partial privatization" scheme. The Republican, former Florida governor Jeb Bush, responded with a vow to succeed where his brother the president had failed by getting a controversial "individual investment accounts" add-on to the Social Security system through a deadlocked Congress and enacted into law. Neither said how he would restore the retirement system's long-term fiscal stability.

When it became clear that the candidates would not discuss specific fiscal remedies without additional prodding, the ACF took to the airwaves again. The second wave began on October 1 and featured separate television ads in which prominent representatives of each major party pointedly asked their own party's nominee why he had not yet endorsed the party's model plan.

Most striking was the Republican ad, which opened with a familiar face voicing a gentle reproach. "Jeb Bush has called for private Social Security investment accounts. But he knows he has to find a way to finance existing Social Security obligations before he can divert FICA money into private accounts. He also knows that some of the best minds in the Republican Party think that the only way to do both is to apply a means test to Social Security, cutting way back on the size of the checks sent to people like me and Bill Gates. It made sense to them and it makes sense to me. Let us know what you think, Jeb!"

The speaker was the candidate's father, the first president Bush, an ACF trustee.

Follow-up polls showed that the public wanted more attention to the issue. Before the candidates could respond, however, the Venezuelan revolution and the Quebec separation crisis erupted within days of each other in mid October, pushing Social Security into the background.

The twin crises sparked a heated campaign debate over future of U.S. policy toward those newly transformed nations. Although hemispheric and other foreign-policy questions dominated the last televised candidate debate on October 20, Social Security was not completely ignored. Bush, in an appeal to independent and democratic voters, pledged to submit Social Security means-testing legislation to Congress after his election. Dean, mindful of his slippage in the polls in the wake of major foreign-policy news, rejected any increase in the capital gains or payroll taxes, arguing that an increase in the retirement age to 70 for those with earnings in the top 55 percent of incomes would make tax increases unnecessary as long as no Social Security revenues were diverted to private investment accounts.

When the returns were in, it became clear that the sudden emergence of a foreign-policy debate kept the election from conclusively resolving the fate of Social Security reform. By elevating national security to the top of the agenda, the debate shifted many votes and the election itself to the Republican candidate.

His slim margin of victory, plus continued public ambivalence toward both partial privatization and means testing, denied the president-elect a clear mandate for his Social Security package, however. Bound by his means-test and privatization pledges but also confronting a Senate unexpectedly back in Democratic hands, the third president Bush returned to the campaign trail in search of fresh support for the package, hoping to do for it what his brother had done for his own signature tax cut after the 2000 election.

When winter and early spring polls continued to show small majorities opposed to both features of the Bush plan, Senate majority leader Tom Daschle declared that the package lacked the votes to pass in that chamber. Bush, determined to avoid an embarrassing defeat on the issue, entered into intense negotiations with the bipartisan leadership in both houses of Congress. In the end, Bush and congressional leaders agreed to table his most controversial proposals but to raise the Social Security tax paid by workers and employees from 6.2 to 7.16 percent, an increase sufficient to keep the system going until 2077. Legislative approval and a Rose Garden bill-signing ceremony followed in June. The president was acclaimed for his bipartisanship and for having crafted a solution to a controversial problem that had long stymied his predecessors.

In retrospect, ACF advertising and polling were credited with helping to nudge the federal government into addressing one of its most controversial problems well before it reached the crisis stage. In a system prone to letting problems fester until crises force action, this was no small achievement. It is far from clear, however, that the newly announced campaign to put health-care reform on the campaign agenda could have a similar impact on the policy debate in the 2012 cycle.[5]

Conclusion

By intervening selectively and intelligently in campaign-policy debates, the proposed American Citizens' Foundation can achieve three beneficial results.

First, it can help make the political debate on the national agenda a less partisan process, not so exclusively driven by ideological zealotry or self-serving electoral calculations.

Next, it can increase the number of future presidents-elect who will have campaigned on concrete proposals addressed to an important policy problem that had a meaningful chance to be explicitly endorsed by the voters.

And, third, it can bring to mass public awareness the best thinking on major national problems. When effective, such exposure can enrich and enlarge an existing public consensus, magnifying its ability to encourage policy action.

Collectively, these will not only increase voter policy influence, but will also increase the chance that controversial issues can be confronted and resolved through the electoral process. Both are necessary if American government is to be both democratic and effective.

Notes

1. Third parties and other novel political ventures provide useful inspiration for the proposal in the text. For one thing, they show that it is entirely possible to do the kind of thing proposed here: use unconventional means to involve the public in ratifying policy. For example, Andrew Jackson's call for a referendum on his Bank veto in the 1832 election and Newt Gingrich's use of the Contract with America to nationalize the 1994 midterm elections illustrate different ways that elections have been used to make the vote more clearly relevant to the endorsement or rejection of policy.

    Perot is the example used in the text, but third parties have a long and significant history of influencing policy because they have attracted popular support in ways that forced a response from major-party candidates (Rosenstone, Behr, and Lazarus 1996). The 1912 election — a contest between the Republican William Howard Taft, Democrat Woodrow Wilson, and the Progressive Party candidate, former Republican president Theodore Roosevelt — has been described as "one of the most substantive presidential campaigns in American history" largely because of the Wilson-Roosevelt debate over the future of reform. Wilson, in his "New Freedom" program, promised tariff reform and action against the trusts to restore competition. Roosevelt "offered the 'New Nationalism' which envisioned a stronger regulatory state and enhanced government power" (Gould 2003, 43).

    Third parties are nevertheless an unpredictable presence with sometimes unintended policy consequences. In the 2000 presidential campaign, for example, Ralph Nader, a self-styled progressive, actually played a large role in the defeat of Democrat Al Gore by siphoning votes away from Gore in Florida and other hotly contested states. By assisting Republican George W. Bush's victory, Nader helped to bring about a significant shift to the right in economic, domestic, and foreign policy. His impact on policy was real enough but inimical to his professed values. In the end, however, it is the uncertainty that third parties will even arise, let alone have the impact that their standard bearers intend, that argues for a less quirky, more institutionalized approach to leveraging voter policy influence.

2. The American Citizen's Foundation was originally conceived and recommended by the 1988 Markle Commission on the Media and the Electorate to pursue a similar though broader public service mission (Buchanan 1991, 157).

3. Two levels of enhanced public influence potentially flowing from ACF interventions can be identified: agency and partnership. Full partnership status as defined here emerges only if the voters contribute to legislative success. Public influence can increase significantly without achieving full partnership status, however. This situation did not arise in the cases already reviewed, but it will be apparent in the hypothetical scenarios presented later in this chapter and in Chapter 6. Influence of a high order is demonstrated, for example, if voters just manage to get an issue on the agenda that would not have been there without their input. That is enough to show that they are causal forces or agents. In what follows, I set partnership as the goal but accept demonstrated agency as an important sign of progress toward it.

4. As Stanley Kelley pointed out more than two decades ago, the technology exists to pinpoint quite precisely the state of voter opinion on policies and candidates (1983). However, the technology has not been commonly used or widely trusted to settle questions such as whether or not poll-tested support for a candidate implies explicit endorsement of that candidate's position on one or more issues (Dahl 1990).

5. References for the Social Security scenario include Baker and Weisbrot (1999); Brock (2003b); and Issues for Debate in American Public Policy (2000).

Chapter 6
The Future of Public Influence:
Revising Health Care

The aim of this concluding chapter is to show in greater detail how the American Citizens' Foundation (ACF) can be usefully deployed in the real world. That, however, will require some prior attention to the policy history of the issue. We choose health care — a controversial issue that, at the time of this writing, remains stubbornly unresolved — because it is a classic policy partnership question: complex, not in full-blown crisis, but of great and increasing personal concern to a large majority of the American people who have waited a long time to get the problem solved.

Despite decades of debate and political struggle, the U.S. healthcare system, the technological envy of the world, has yet to overcome the lower cost–greater access advantages enjoyed by other less high-tech but fully national healthcare systems like those found in Canada and several European countries. In fact, the United States remains the only industrial democracy in the world that does not have national health insurance (Gordon 2003). It is understandable, then, that despite repeated failure to muster winning political support in Washington for national insurance, the American people still evince strong support (67 percent) for "the government guaranteeing health care for all citizens" (*http://people-press.org/reports/pdf/190.pdf*).

This strong support of American citizens for national health care may help explain why the most politically difficult option — a government-regulated single-payer national health insurance system — recently pushed its way to the surface once again. Arguing that the $294.3 billion that Americans were estimated to have spent on health care in 1999 equalled $1,059 a patient, compared to just $307 in Canada, the nonprofit

Physicians for a National Health Program called for a government-sponsored national health insurance program that would provide medical coverage for all Americans. Their August 2003 proposal, endorsed by some 8,000 of the group's members, was based on a study conducted by researchers at the Harvard Medical School and published in the *New England Journal of Medicine*. The study's lead author, Harvard Medical School Associate Professor Stephie Woolhandler, said that the savings gained from a national health insurance system like Canada's, in which the government is the single payer of healthcare costs, would be enough to provide for the 41 million Americans who lack coverage (Lueck 2003, D2; Pereira 2003, D3). By eliminating the high overhead and profits of the private, investor-owned insurance industry and reducing spending for marketing and other related services, national health care costs would be reduced by nearly $200 billion a year. Dr. Quentin Young, national coordinator for the physicians group, claimed other advantages as well: "Universal health insurance is associated with better health care outcomes — life expectancy is longer, freedom from preventable disease, [and better rates of] infant mortality and maternal mortality" (quoted in Wynn 2003, A6).

Unsurprisingly, the proposal attracted influential critics. One, Henry Aaron of the Brookings Institution (Pereira 2003, D3), questioned the objectivity of the researchers, who are long-known advocates of a national health insurance system. He also suggested that the study's authors may have exaggerated U.S. healthcare costs by as much as 24 percent because the research doesn't take into account such things as labor and standard-of-living costs, which are much higher in the United States than in Canada. In a radio interview shortly after the Harvard study appeared, Aaron pointed out that it is not an accident that the United States has the healthcare system it has. The existing system reflects a long and difficult political struggle. Changing anything as entrenched as the U.S. healthcare system, and changing it as drastically as the single-payer proposal would do, would be enormously difficult, if not impossible.

In an editorial in the same issue of the New England Journal of Medicine, the American Medical Association (AMA), which publishes the journal, also voiced strong disagreement with the single-payer proposal. AMA president Donald Palmisano (Lueck 2003, D2) said that under a single-payer system the United States would be trading one problem for many others, such as long waits for services, a slowness to adopt new technologies and maintain facilities, and development of a large bureaucracy that could cause a decline in the authority of patients and their physicians over clinical decision making.

Fundamental disagreements like these run through the discussions that follow, from the brief historical overview presented next, to the descriptions of the model partisan healthcare reform options currently most favored by Democratic and Republican policy experts, to the fictional scenarios that detail the ACF strategy for bringing the voters more directly into the business of setting American healthcare policy. Helping the American people to resolve such disagreements by choosing between options clarified during presidential election seasons is exactly what the ACF is designed to do.

Background

The fact that the latest national healthcare proposal comes from a group of physicians is especially noteworthy because the medical profession, together with business interests, have traditionally been the two most powerful *opponents* of the kind of compulsory national health insurance proposed mainly by progressives and labor interests throughout the twentieth century. To date, the forces of opposition have triumphed. National health plans proposed by presidents Franklin D. Roosevelt in 1939, Harry S. Truman in 1948, and Bill Clinton in 1993 all failed to win congressional approval.

Many do not realize that the U.S. healthcare system now in place emerged quite late in our national history, not taking shape until the 1950s and 1960s. Before that, people were essentially left to their own devices. Due to evolving economic circumstances, however, employers saw reason (competition for workers) to begin offering private health insurance. An unforeseeable political event (the Kennedy assassination) put a legislative master, Lyndon B. Johnson, in a position to enact in 1965 the two major programs that still anchor the federal government healthcare system: Medicare and Medicaid. The bills were passed despite the continuing opposition of the medical profession in a "brief moment of liberal triumph" (Jost 2000, 48).

By the late 1960s workplace insurance had evolved to the point that approximately two-thirds of the population had at least hospitalization insurance as part of their employee-benefits packages. Even with a large chunk of the preretirement, elderly, and poor populations covered, however, it became apparent that the evolving patchwork of private and government systems left many without adequate healthcare coverage. The problem was that many who could not afford to pay for medical care out of their pockets were not eligible for existing workplace or government coverage.

That led political liberals to press once again for broader national health insurance. That in turn prompted a free-enterprise response, this time from the administration of Richard M. Nixon. The Nixon response was codified in the Health Maintenance Organization Act of 1973, which required all businesses with more than twenty-five employees to offer at least one health maintenance organization (HMO) as an alternative to conventional insurance. HMOs are associations of healthcare providers who contract with defined groups of enrollees to deliver specified, prepaid medical services, as an alternative to the traditional "fee-for-service" arrangement traditionally favored by the mainstream medical profession.

By 1995 some 150 million people nationwide were members of such managed-care programs. The programs would be credited with keeping down the rate of cost increases through such practices as regulating doctors' fees and services and disallowing patient access to costly treatments of questionable necessity, but both patients and doctors increasingly bridled under restrictions that put cost containment above improving patient care.

That brings us to the present, where still-increasing costs, plus unhappiness with HMO restrictions and exploding numbers of people with no healthcare insurance, signal an urgent need for reform. Despite the relative success of the cost controls introduced by managed care, the United States faces seemingly uncontrollable growth in both overall costs and the number of uninsured people. Current estimates put the number of uninsured at 41 million, with the number sometimes swelling to 60 million or more as those between jobs temporarily lose their insurance (Pear 2003a, A20).

The problem continues to grow in part because special interests — mainly political and economic interests — have blocked efforts to improve a system that benefits them at the expense of the American people as a whole (Johnson and Broder 1996). It is also the case that the technical and financial problems are quite daunting, with no easy answers. The vested stakeholders have not stepped forward to clarify the real policy choices in light of those problems, however; instead, they have clouded the debate and obscured the real choices with a steady diet of self-serving rhetoric. That, in the end, explains why the *political* debate over alternative solutions has not yet produced the clarity needed to inspire corrective action.

The Clinton Initiative

It is helpful to understand the "deep background" of the American healthcare dilemma, but the history most relevant to the task before us is more recent. I refer to the unsuccessful 1993 Clinton healthcare initiative.

In the American competitive political system, the fight for power forces candidates to espouse policies that they believe will maximize their electoral prospects. That is why Bill Clinton, as a 1992 presidential candidate who promised a national healthcare system during the campaign, wanted no part of a tax-funded government-regulated national healthcare plan like those found in Canada, Italy, and the United Kingdom. His reading of the political climate led him to opt instead for an employer-mandated managed-care approach, regulated but not controlled by the government. He was committed to using the government, but only in a way consistent with his "New Democrat" philosophy, which favored incorporating the private sector and economic competition into government policy and avoiding new taxes or a heavy reliance on regulation. This philosophy stemmed from his experience as governor of Arkansas and from his political struggle to distance himself from the label of "tax and spend" Democrat (Hacker 1997). The Clinton proposal would be consistent with the market-friendly, no-new-taxes New Democrat philosophy he saw as the road to the White House.

The Plan

The underlying concept, known as *pay-or-play*, was devised as a way to keep much of the existing insurance system intact while also expanding coverage. The basic provision was simple: each business would be given a choice of providing insurance for its own workers, with part of the cost deducted from workers' pay and part from the employer (as is the current practice), or contributing to a national healthcare insurance fund administered by the government that would organize to purchase private insurance for those who could not get it from an employer (Johnson and Broder 1996, 75).

Clinton made it abundantly clear in his campaign book *Putting People First*, published in June 1992, and in a September 1992 campaign speech that he preferred a liberal version of "managed competition" that would establish universal access to health insurance by requiring employers to contribute to their employees' insurance and by creating new regional bodies that would negotiate with private health plans and monitor competition between them. Thus, despite an elaborate postelection task force that some mistakenly saw as the source of his proposal (the task force was actually intended only to build consensus within the fractious health policy community and to signal apolitical "expert" endorsement in hopes of making the Clinton plan more credible to the public), the measure sent to Congress was consistent with the intentions that Clinton had long since made clear on the campaign trail (Jacobs and Shapiro 2000, 79–80).

The Legislative Strategy

In part because he believed that public opinion was separate from "what would sell in Congress," Clinton made no systematic effort to cultivate public support for use as leverage (Jacobs and Shapiro 2000, 97). Instead, he focused most of his attention on the "inside game," working to get his plan past the various ideological gatekeepers on Capital Hill (Jacobs and Shapiro 2000, 83).

Clinton's adoption of a complex and comprehensive managed-care proposal resulted from his own policy goals but also from his political judgment that this proposal would unite a coalition of disparate elements within the Democratic and Republican Congressional parties.

Clinton hoped, too, that both economic and healthcare issues could be addressed simultaneously as part of his effort to get the budget deficit under control. For that reason, and also in the hope of bypassing the legislative roadblocks associated with the filibuster and unlimited debate, he tried (unsuccessfully) to get Senate Appropriations Committee Chairman Robert Byrd to incorporate healthcare reform into the expedited budget-reconciliation process (Johnson and Broder 1996, 125). When that failed, Clinton did not reach out to Senate Republicans and moderate Democrats who had proposed their own healthcare reforms, as a prudent inside player would have done; instead, he continued to lobby in Congress for his own proposal. In his 1994 State of the Union message, Clinton further discouraged potential compromise by pledging to veto any bill that would not guarantee a short timetable to achieve universal coverage. At that point, a united public, clamoring for legislative action on health care, would have been very useful. As noted, however, Clinton had not conceived his legislative task in a way that relied on the public.

Public Opinion

Other reasons existed for why the president had not made public support a centerpiece of his legislative strategy. One was that he simply assumed that he would be able to evoke a generally supportive public reaction whenever it might prove useful. The most important reason, however, may have been his reluctance to share control over the content of his plan for reform.

Clinton put health care at the top of his agenda not because there was strong public support for a new approach (there was), but because he and his advisers identified it as the means for achieving his overriding goals of economic rejuvenation and deficit reduction (Hacker 1997). He was therefore unmoved by the fact that a plan like the Canadian-inspired single-payer system, a decidedly "old Democrat" approach to the problem in Clinton's mind, enjoyed significant support among the public and "upwards of a third of congressional Democrats." Nor was he moved by the fact that Americans were willing to support a direct and explicit payroll tax to finance the new system, an approach more popular than the employer-mandate approach Clinton preferred (Jacobs and Shapiro 2000, 81, 98).

Although they were not the focal point of his legislative strategy, Clinton did make some efforts to encourage a supportive public. He spoke to the nation often on the subject of health care, and the White House mounted a public-relations effort that resembled a political campaign, driven by "the same polling and media consultants who had steered the 1992 presidential campaign." Johnson and Broder (1996) saw this as over-politicization, arguing that the "entire mind-set of the Clinton White House was to treat the passage of health care reform as the campaign of 1994." This way of going public was a fateful step, because it invited the opposition to use the same tactics (614–15). That is exactly what the opposition did, mounting its own countercampaign that ultimately brought the Clinton initiative to ruin.

What Went Wrong?

Many causes for the meltdown of the Clinton healthcare bill have been suggested. These causes include the president's decision to put his wife Hillary in charge of the healthcare venture (Johnson and Broder1996); overreliance on secret task forces to develop the legislative proposal (Gutmann and Thompson 1996); failure to reach across the partisan divide vigorously enough, plus failure to enlist the help of Democratic barons like Senators Daniel Patrick Moynihan of New York and Sam Nunn of Georgia (Johnson and Broder 1996); failure to take into account the huge economic magnitude of the proposed policy (12 percent of a $3 trillion economy — see Marmor 1994); and the drag imposed by the budget deficit inherited from the Reagan and first Bush administrations (Skocpol 1997).

Each of these factors no doubt contributed to the demise of the Clinton healthcare plan, but the decisive factor was most likely issuing a veto threat that drove potential supporters into opposition before having "locked in" public demand for healthcare legislation. Had Clinton made it a priority to establish a strong bond with the public on the issue before the legislative struggle began, the outcome might well have been different. Such a bond would have been facilitated, for example, by a tighter, more exclusive, and more pedagogical focus on the healthcare issue during the campaign (the Clinton campaign pressed far too many issues for any one to stand out clearly). It is also possible that a well-publicized modification of his plan, in deference to clear public preferences, would have increased the public's sense of identification with what was ultimately proposed and debated in Congress. Clinton might then have been in a stronger position to do what Reagan did for his tax cuts: ask the people to flood Congress with evidence of their insistence that a healthcare plan be enacted into law. Because Clinton did not do these or other things that might have served to entrench public opinion on his side of the policy debate, however, he failed to capitalize effectively on public enthusiasm for health care. That left a vital political resource — public support — up for grabs.

The Anti-Policy Coalition

A coalition made up of opposition Republicans and special-interest lobbies such as the Health Insurance Association of America and the National Federation of Independent Business then used the airwaves and opinion pages to attack the Clinton healthcare plan. The reaction to that well-financed and well-coordinated attack campaign built what amounted to a veto partnership with the public that proved decisive in defeating the Clinton plan (Johnson and Broder 1996, 628–29).

Because President Clinton did not have a preemptive strategy for binding the public to his cause (and because there was no nonpartisan help from an outside source like the American Citizens' Foundation to help counter the misinformation spread by special-interest attack advertising), he left the field wide open to Harry and Louise, the couple made famous in TV ads paid for by the opposition coalition.

Conclusion: Polarization Encourages Sabotage

By mounting an effective ad campaign, the opposition coalition mobilized public opinion against "Hillary-care," as they dubbed it, winning an impressive political victory. Far less praiseworthy, however, was the fact that the healthcare problem was left unsolved, and the very idea of universal coverage was discredited for more than a decade. That raises an important question: why weren't congressional Republicans motivated to seek a compromise solution to the problem? Why was defeating the Clinton initiative more important than replacing it with something better?

A proposition suggested by this and other recent experiences is that ideological polarization encourages political sabotage rather than compromise. Clinton, in a decision he later regretted, had embraced a purely partisan approach to getting his initial budget enacted in 1993, succeeding without a single Republican vote. His failure to invite Republicans into the budget debate encouraged them to embrace a similarly uncompromising attitude toward the healthcare plan. With political elites now more ideologically polarized than at any time since the turn of the twentieth century (Cameron 2002), opposition parties are more prone to treat governing party proposals like the Clinton healthcare plan — or, to cite a more recent example from the other side, judicial nominations like the second President Bush's choice of Miguel Estrada to serve as the first Hispanic judge on the U.S. Court of Appeals for the District of Columbia — as opportunities to advance political agendas. "The fight over Mr. Estrada's nomination was the most prominent and most protracted battle in what has become a nasty ideological and political war with no end in sight between the White House and Senate Democrats over who gets to sit on the federal bench" (Lewis 2003, 1).

It is very difficult for the political system to deal effectively with complex issues like health care, let alone the politics of judicial nominations, if their fate is controlled by partisans more interested in political victory than in compromise solutions. Many believe that such partisanship has gone too far. For example, both Democrats and Republicans were recently taken to task for their self-serving mismanagement of the long-standing debate over fiscal policy. New York Federal Reserve Bank chair and former Nixon Commerce Secretary Pete Peterson, a founding member of the bipartisan antideficit Concord Coalition, sees an alarming erosion of concern for the common good:

> What exactly gave rise to this bipartisan flight from integrity and responsibility — and when? My own theory, for what it's worth, is

that it got started during the "Me Decade," the 1970's, when a socially fragmented America began to gravitate around a myriad of interest groups, each more fixated on pursuing and financing, through massive political campaign contributions, its own agenda than on safeguarding the common good of the nation. Political parties, rather than helping to transcend these fissures and bind the country together, instead began to cater to them and ultimately sold themselves out. … I'm not sure what it will take to make our two-party system healthy again. I hope that in the search for a durable majority, the Republicans will sooner or later realize that it won't happen without coming to terms with deficits and debts, and Democrats will likewise realize it won't happen for them without coming to terms with Entitlements. (2003, 15)

What Peterson deplores may be inevitable. Unless forced by public opinion to do otherwise, parties, campaign organizations, candidates, and presidents will often put their narrow political interests above "safeguarding the common good."

When polarized partisans dominate the public debate, fair-minded analysis gets pushed aside by self-serving spin, leaving the people to sort out the facts with little real help from the media portrayal of the spectacle. Although President Clinton made many tactical errors in pressing his initiative, and deserves much of the responsibility that he publicly accepted for the failure of his plan, the coalition arrayed against him mounted a $50 million public-relations campaign that discredited the plan before the public understood it.

Health Care in 2004

A decade after the Clinton failure, the piecemeal incremental approach then touted as the most feasible has again been found wanting. Universal healthcare coverage was back on the table, at least among the Democratic Party candidates during the run-up to the 2004 presidential election campaign.

The Democrats were responding to the fact that public dissatisfaction with health care was intensifying. In a May 2003 *New York Times/CBS News* poll, for example, "88 percent of respondents said the nation's healthcare system needed fundamental change or a complete overhaul, and by a margin of 51 to 29 percent, they said the Democratic Party was better equipped than the Republicans to do the job" (Nagourney and Elder 2003, A1; Nagourney 2003b; A12). The August 2003 Pew poll cited in Chapter 5 showed that 67 percent favored government-guaranteed health care for all, even if it meant raising taxes or repealing tax cuts. Also in August, 8,000 members of Physicians for a National Health Program issued the call, discussed earlier, for a national single-payer health insurance program that would provide medical coverage for all Americans. With the economy slumping and polls showing health care to be of increasing concern to the American people, it was inevitable that the Democratic hopefuls would try to resurrect the issue (Polman 2003, A11).

Candidate Positions

The first candidate to respond was former Vermont governor and physician Howard Dean, who proposed universal health care as a policy goal. Soon, all the other major Democratic candidates had embraced the goal of universal coverage. At first they generally advocated just limited steps in that direction, such as allowing parents of low-income children and those aged 55 to 64 to obtain coverage under Medicaid, the federal–state healthcare program for the poor, and Medicare, the federal program for the elderly and disabled (Harwood 2003a, A4). Later, Rep. Dick Gephardt (D-Mo.), in a bid to jump-start his then-lagging campaign, declared that "access to quality health care is the moral issue of our time." He proposed that the much-criticized Bush tax cuts be rescinded so as to finance a program of healthcare subsidies for employers that, Gephardt said, would cover 97 percent of the 41 million currently uninsured. He claimed that it would cost $692 billion over the first three years, which he would finance by repealing the $1.35 trillion tax-cut plan passed by Congress in 2002 and by rejecting the new round of tax cuts proposed by President Bush in 2003. The plan would effectively require every business to provide subsidized healthcare insurance for its employees and to provide employees with federal tax credits equivalent to the cost of 60 percent of the premiums to defray the costs (Nagourney 2003a, A26). Soon, all of the Democratic candidates had plans with varying details. Following Gephardt's lead, however, they were united in offering the public a political trade-off: better health care versus the Bush tax cuts. All candidates would finance their plans by either partially or fully repealing the tax cuts (Lipman 2003, A17).

For his part, President Bush hoped to reduce the appeal of the Democrats' healthcare proposals by signing (on November 25, 2003) a prescription drug bill before the election, a $400 billion measure that represented the largest expansion of Medicare since its 1965 creation.

The fates of the Democratic candidates and their healthcare proposals were unknown at the time this was written. There was always the chance that the stars would align to generate a campaign that featured a substantial healthcare debate, but that seemed unlikely. The 2004 campaign was unfolding in ways that pointed away from a focus on health care and toward a referendum on Bush's performance in his first term.

If it shows nothing else, our brief passage through the history of the healthcare debate shows conclusively why the issue is so ripe for an intervention like that described in Chapter 5. The problem is complex, political opponents remain contentious, the public is calling for action, and yet that same public has been and could easily again be misled in a way that prevents a national decision to implement a compromise solution.

The antidote to disinformation is the kind of bipartisan healthcare conference held in the spring of 2003 at the Lyndon Baines Johnson Library in Austin, Texas. The conference so closely matched the recommended first step of the ACF process set out in Chapter 5 that it could have been designed for that purpose. The mandate is to "ask the best experts to develop the fairest possible descriptions of a national problem that voters identify as among the most important facing the country. The same experts will then be asked to generate realistic partisan options for solving the problem, options that reflect the most influential Republican and Democratic policy thinking." That, in essence, is what happened.

Bipartisan Policy Analysis

Entitled "Big Choices: The Future of Health Insurance for America's Families," the symposium, which assembled at the Lyndon Baines Johnson Library and School of Public Affairs at the University of Texas at Austin on April 25, 2003, drew leading healthcare policy experts from all sides of the political spectrum, including academics, national, state, and local government officials, and interest-group leaders.

The substance of what was said about the healthcare problem and the options before us are excerpted in the fictional scenarios that follow. Here, our aim is to convey the spirit of this symposium and its fit with the ideal of an informed electorate. Both were nicely captured in a remark by one panelist, the Urban Institute's Alan Weil, a seasoned participant in the healthcare wars at both state and federal levels, during the concluding roundtable discussion.

Weil noted that the symposium atmosphere was a refreshing departure from the usually politicized healthcare policy debates in Washington. Healthcare arguments inside the Beltway, he said, feature symbolic posturing — with one side claiming that expanding federal benefits would only spike big government, and the other saying that antigovernment solutions disrespect the needs of the disadvantaged. He, at least, found it refreshing that there was less posturing at this conference, precisely because it was not so politicized.

The conference featured the views of many strong-willed people, all of whom have explored this issue in depth from various political angles, clarified the basic problems, and proposed workable solutions. Two clear options were presented, as was a proposal to compromise by synthesizing the two. All stopped short of universal coverage, as the participants remained convinced that there were neither the funds nor the political support yet in place for a comprehensive solution.

If the symposium clarified the options in a way that could be helpful to the public, however, it also demonstrated once again that the ideological disagreements over solutions are not close to being resolved. Despite the fact that (as another participant in the concluding roundtable discussion put it) "many of us have been having this conversation for twenty five years," the partners have yet to reach a clear consensus on what to do.

Although there are many side issues and embroideries that we will not consider here, the fundamental deadlock remains the same: One side favors market solutions, such as tax credits or vouchers, and the other side prefers federal-government solutions based on the Medicare and Medicaid models. So far, at least, the compromise proposals that try to combine the two have not bred much consensus.

The symposium's prognosis for future action was guarded. Some participants said that we cannot expect to solve this problem until it reaches crisis proportions. Others said that a decision cannot be reached without involving the public, and that one way to do that is by getting high-profile public figures that have a chance to pass legislation to ask for public attention and explain the alternatives.

Interestingly, no one mentioned election campaigns. That was clearly not their frame of reference. By "involving the public," participants meant things like public hearings such as group panels that had taken place in Colorado and other states, or focus groups, such as had been run by several state officials in the roundtable. One reason the conference participants did not think immediately of a campaign as a place to frame and settle the question is because most agreed with Weil's observation that campaigns are run on the Washington, D.C. model, where the aim is to posture and make debating points, not to clarify choices in preparation for publicly ratified decision and action.

Campaign Shortcomings

A typical presidential campaign has additional problems from the perspective of a complex and controversial issue like health care. One is that a proposal that can survive the primary season and that does not prevent a general election win is generally one that stresses benefits with little or no attention to costs and is therefore incomplete. That is a fair description of the Clinton plan as a campaign proposal. An election debate that ignores costs cannot offer much in the way of ratification for a subsequent legislative proposal, which cannot avoid them.

Another campaign-related disadvantage is that the winner's proposal is not likely to have been tested against an alternative proposal put forward by opponent(s) in the general election. The most recent example, the Clinton healthcare proposal, drew no serious response from either George H.W. Bush or Ross Perot in the 1992 presidential campaign.

A third problem is that few campaigns permit either the isolation or the focus needed to clarify a complicated issue. Given the multitopic blur that most campaigns become, the debate is unlikely to communicate either the expert consensus on the nature of the problem and the major alternative solutions, or to publicize the impact on public opinion that exposure to such information can have.

Revising Health Care

How might we address these campaign shortcomings as well as the tendencies toward polarization, disinformation, and deadlock? What follows is an effort to provide some answers. We began the story in the fictional newspaper article dated August 15, 2011, that closed Chapter 5. There, please recall, the ACF had announced its intention to try to make health-care reform a "policy partnership" issue for the 2012 presidential election. The story continues in another newspaper article as the 2012 primary season is getting under way.

ELECTION FOUNDATION PRESSES HEALTH CARE AGENDA

Dateline: Hanover, Hew Hampshire, February 3, 2012

Hoping to attract many of the hundreds of reporters in town to cover Tuesday's first-in-the-nation presidential primary, the American Citizens' Foundation held a press briefing yesterday to promote its ongoing campaign to put health care atop the 2012 election agenda.

Heartened by its modest share of the credit for the bipartisan compromise that produced the Social Security Reform Act of 2009, the group now hopes to enlist the public in an effort to make the health care issue the centerpiece of what is shaping up to be hotly competitive race for both the Democratic Party nomination and the White House.

The ACF began pressing the 2012 candidates to embrace the issue last August. So far, neither surprise Iowa Caucuses winner Senator Hillary Rodham Clinton (D-N.Y.) nor New Hampshire frontrunner Senator John Edwards (D-N.C.) has made health care a top priority. But the ACF's ambitious national advertising campaign has apparently made some headway with voters. Polls predating last summer's ACF campaign launching showed that a plurality of Americans — 25 percent in a July Gallup Poll — already regarded the twin concerns of healthcare access and cost as "the most important problem facing the country." The most recent surveys indicate that concern is increasing. The issue currently ranks third behind the latest crisis on the Korean Peninsula and inflation, both of which have recently dominated the news.

The health care debate has been marked by intense ideological conflict for the past two decades. Following the Republican defeat of the Clinton administration's universal coverage initiative in 1994, private-sector employer-provided insurance that featured managed-care programs such as HMOs and preferred provider organizations (PPOs) increased in importance. By the end of the 1990s such programs had expanded to cover more than 150 million people nationwide. Managed care was credited with helping to bring down the rate of increase in health care costs. But both doctors and patients complained about cost-cutting pressures and denial of services by program administrators. Meanwhile, increasingly expensive premiums, cutbacks in employer coverage, and cyclic spikes in the unemployment rate sometimes swelled the ranks of the uninsured above 60 million people.

Competition for the votes of seniors led to the largest expansion of Medicare since its 1965 inception in 2003 when overlapping $400 billion bills approving prescription drug assistance passed each house of Congress. The bill was signed into law on November 25, 2003, but questions about its costs, plus ongoing concern with the millions of uninsured Americans, kept the issue alive.

Since 2003, affordability and access problems have continued to worsen, as have the prospects for bipartisan compromise. Bush Republicans kept control of the White House in 2004 and 2008, but a razor-thin margin of Republican control of Congress after 2004 and the narrow capture of the Senate by Democrats in 2008 have prevented significant movement on either prescription drugs for seniors, the growing number of uninsured, or spiraling healthcare costs. At the press briefing, foundation spokesperson Olympia Snowe pointed to this gridlock as the principal reason the ACF chose health care as the focus of a new issue campaign.

The policy briefs, as the foundation calls the television infomercials and shorter advertisements it sponsors, reflect its staunchly bipartisan, problem-solving ethos (transcripts are available at *policypartnership.org*). The most detailed presentation, a fifteen-minute infomercial that ran on various networks and cable channels at least once each week throughout the fall of 2011, described the problem and set out model Democratic and Republican proposals for solving it. Both were derived from ACF-sponsored conferences at which both nonpartisan experts and specialists associated with liberal and conservative think tanks discussed and debated the issues. There was bipartisan agreement on three key issues: that universal coverage of the sort attempted by the Clinton administration was still not politically feasible; that the goal was to expand healthcare access and affordability in large but still incremental steps; and that government-financed subsidies are needed in order to take such steps. The sticking point was over how the subsidies should be provided.

The options included in the model candidate proposals advertised by the ACF differ mainly in the extent of their reliance on government management and control of the subsidies. The model Republican plan, for example, features tax credits or vouchers that can reach half or more of the uninsured population by helping eligible individuals to pay private health insurance premiums, with little direct government involvement. The model Democratic plan, on the other hand, recommends expanding the existing Federal-State Medicaid and State Children's Health Insurance Program (SCHIP) systems to make them available to all low-income adults, who comprise more than half of the uninsured population.

Former Senator Snowe, the ACF spokesperson, affirmed that if a serious debate on the healthcare issue had not begun by the time the nominees were chosen and the fall campaign was underway, her group would again mobilize its highest-profile trustees to try to ratchet up the pressure on the candidates.[1]

As noted in the article, the ACF broadcast a fifteen-minute infomercial "at least once each week" during the fall of 2011. The purpose was to inform and strengthen the original voter consensus on the importance of the healthcare problem, as well as to acquaint the electorate with the model partisan options also described in the article. The tone of the presentation — particularly the way it seeks to motivate the audience to accept an agenda-setting and a decision-making role in the debate by putting pressure on candidates to address the issue — is suggested by the following excerpts from the infomercial.

INFOMERCIAL TRANSCRIPT, FALL 2011

Moderator: This is a public service message from your organization and mine, the American Citizens' Foundation. As a Canadian who became a naturalized citizen of the United States, I am especially proud to be an American, not least because of the "can do" spirit with which my adopted country confronts and solves its problems.

The problem I wish to discuss with you today is one that many of you have identified as among the most important facing the country: health care. Polls show that a majority of Americans believe the government should do something to make sure that every American has access to affordable, high-quality health care. The Congress has been split down the middle on the healthcare issue for years, and the time has come for you the people to help them decide. The way to do that is to elect a president who is committed to a plan that makes sense to you.

The presentation you are about to see has three purposes. The first is to explain the healthcare problem in a way that is clear and fair to all sides.

The second is to highlight the major differences between two alternative plans developed by experts from our two major political parties so that you can decide which one is best for our country. The third purpose is to ask for your help in getting each of the major party nominees for president to take a stand on health care by endorsing either the Republican or the Democratic plan.

As for the problem, here is what the best experts from the universities and the two major political parties concluded after a series of meetings to study the healthcare problem at the Bush and Johnson presidential libraries in Texas.

All agreed that something must be done to begin the process of extending coverage to the more than 50 million people who now have no healthcare insurance. All agree that out-of-control healthcare costs must be reined in. And most agree that government subsidies will be required to get it done. But there was strong disagreement between the two parties on the best way to proceed.

The Democratic Party experts say that the most rational and moral first step is to expand the existing Medicaid and State Child Health Insurance programs to cover all low-income adults. The Republican experts, on the other hand, say it is best to encourage responsibility by giving tax credits and vouchers to individuals to help them buy their own health insurance in the marketplace.

Each plan would be financed by government subsidies, thus lowering the cost of health care. Each would cost roughly the same amount of money to implement. And each would reach about half of the uninsured population, as big a step as both sides think can be taken at this time.

What are the major differences? The Democratic plan targets the lowest income portion of the uninsured population and relies on expanding existing government programs to reach them. By comparison, the Republican program limits the government role to funding vouchers and asks eligible people to make their own insurance arrangements. Initially at least, those most able and willing to make these arrangements, people who are usually not among the lowest-income portion of the uninsured population, are the likeliest beneficiaries.

Here is where you, the voters, come in. Polls show that a large number of you want this problem solved, one way or another. But the long history of deadlock in Congress suggests that it won't be solved unless you, the American people, come together to insist. The first and most important step, therefore, is to send the presidential candidates a message. The message is that we want them to take the pledge to get this problem solved.

We ask that you write, call, or e-mail your favorite presidential candidate asking her or him to endorse one or another of these model plans and to promise to submit it to Congress if elected President. If enough of us do that, we can be sure that the Republican and Democratic Party nominees for president will both be committed to submitting the winning plan to Congress after Inauguration Day and fighting to get it enacted into law.

We will not all agree about which plan is better. But we all do share an interest in using our vote for president to help get a decision made. What better way to show the promise of democracy than by using our votes to get the people we send to Washington to solve big problems like health care?

As noted, this ad ran weekly in September, October, and November of 2011. Thereafter, between the New Hampshire primary and Election Day 2012, the ACF deployed the strategy described in Chapter 5: extensive advertising to keep public opinion in play as pressure mounted on candidates to focus on the healthcare issue and take the pledge. The story of this effort, including an account of how the ACF coped with inevitable surprises, is told in the following fictional retrospective.

ANOTHER SPLIT DECISION FOR AMERICAN CITIZEN'S FOUNDATION

Dateline — Washington, D.C., December 15, 2012

The American Citizen's Foundation, a bipartisan group founded in 2005 to increase the importance of public opinion in presidential campaign policy debates, has now completed two presidential campaign "interventions," as the group calls its signature ventures. The first, mounted in advance of the 2008 presidential campaign, succeeded in raising the profile of the Social Security funding issue enough to have won them some of the credit for prompting Congress to pass the Social Security Reform Act of 2009. That emboldened the ACF to try again this year. But not long after the election, some members of their board of directors are wondering if they did the right thing.

Their target issue — healthcare reform — did get more attention during the 2012 presidential campaign than many expected, given that the nation was caught in an economic downturn that threatened an incumbent's reelection. But it is not clear that health care was featured because of ACF efforts. Although President Jeb Bush lost to Democratic challenger Hillary Rodham Clinton by a popular vote margin of 52 to 48, it is far from certain that the Democratic plan will carry the day.

Two developments explain this unexpected turn of events. The first was that President Bush, with his reelection in jeopardy, pushed the healthcare issue as hard as the ACF did. But despite tilting more toward the Democratic than the Republican model during the campaign, in defeat he has privately encouraged Republican leaders in Congress to oppose the Democratic plan. Second, it is not at all clear that President-elect Clinton, who steadfastly refused to pledge her support for any plan during the campaign, will accept the ACF's postelection offer of help in pushing the voters' choice (the Democratic plan) through a Congress in which the upper chamber is once again in Republican hands.

These complications might have been avoided had the ACF heeded advice to avoid campaigns that featured an incumbent seeking reelection. It decided to continue its intervention at least into the primary season when President Bush, hoping to give his uncertain reelection prospects an early boost, responded to the fall 2011 ACF advertising with a surprise October 15 announcement that he would take the pledge to submit legislation if reelected, but that it would be a mix of the two model plans. Pleased ACF leaders decided that the potential advantages of an early presidential endorsement of their efforts made the problems that could arise in an incumbent race worth risking.

Mindful of the assist he received in 2008 from ACF pressure on the Social Security issue and already aware of Clinton's dislike for the pressure tactics embodied in the fall infomercial, President Bush hoped to claim the healthcare issue as his own and use it to deflect attention from the economic downturn that threatened his hold on the White House. But the ACF faced another difficult decision when Clinton unexpectedly announced, just two days after President Bush's October speech, her refusal to embrace the Democratic model or to take the pledge. Although Clinton was tied with John Edwards in national polls for the Democratic Party nomination in the months before the primary season, the issue-group considered aborting its intervention after her announcement because she was a strong party favorite in early caucus and primary states and widely considered to be the probable nominee. In the end, the ACF brain trust felt compelled to stay the course in order to avoid the impression of weakness in the face of candidate criticism, especially that levied by a prominent Democrat. (The ACF has battled charges by conservative Republicans that its progressive "good government" agenda gives it a liberal bias despite the presence of prominent moderate Republicans on its board.)

The hope was that Clinton would eventually see reason to fall into line. For example, early ACF polling showed a public preference for the

Democratic model. The healthcare issue traditionally has benefited Democrats. And there was the prospect of snatching the issue back from President Bush, leaving him that much more vulnerable to the economic bad news. But as the primaries gave way to the summer nominating conventions, Clinton held her ground. Even the gentle critical pressure voiced by Democratic Party luminaries such as former Vice President Al Gore (from her husband's administration) and Lucy Johnson (daughter of Lyndon Johnson, the president who enacted Medicare) in ACF television advertising failed to draw a response. Despite her refusal to embrace health care, Clinton moved into the post–Labor Day campaign with a substantial lead over President Bush in the polls.

When a desperate President Bush attacked her for refusing to engage the healthcare issue during their single nationally televised debate on the anniversary of his pledge, Clinton deftly turned the criticism against him. She said that the election campaign was about the president's failed economic leadership. He should be required to answer for that and not be given an opportunity to change the subject by attacking any proposal that she might make before Election Day. Therefore, she would offer a healthcare plan after the election, and seek the support of the people before presenting it to Congress.

With the election over, it is clear that Mrs. Clinton's decision to resist the pressure mounted by both the ACF and her opponent was politically well advised. She and her strategy-adviser husband, the former President Clinton, had concluded early on that it was not in her electoral interest to engage the healthcare debate during the campaign. Sources say that the president-elect was also not in sympathy with the ACF approach and resented the pressure brought to bear on her by its advertising.

Reports of Mrs. Clinton's displeasure with the ACF concept had surfaced as early as the summer of 2011, but once she had won the election her attitude encouraged a spate of new and largely critical media commentary. A common theme was that an elitist newcomer institution meddling in an already complex political process was not only presumptuous but potentially harmful, as the unexpected candidate reactions to the latest intervention suggested. Nor was Mrs. Clinton the only presidential candidate to have expressed resentment at the "we know best" attitude implied by efforts to influence their campaigns. Others argued that the ACF has achieved nothing that established parties and candidates could not have done on their own. Still others complained that filling the airwaves with even more advocacy advertising only added to public confusion and general distaste for politics.

What may keep the ACF idea alive, however, is the fact that while those caught in its sights are often displeased, the people remain supportive. Even postelection polling sponsored by unsympathetic interests show that the ACF is still popular with a majority of Americans. In focus groups sponsored by this newspaper to uncover the reasons for this support, people said that what they most appreciated was nonpartisan "briefing" ads that cut through the usual attacks and distortions to help voters compare the candidates on a big issue like health care. They also liked the idea of being asked, at least occasionally, to help set policy. "We can't be in on everything" said a Maryland woman who participated in one of the sessions. "But on an issue like health care, why shouldn't the American people have a voice?"

WITH PRESIDENT FINALLY ON BOARD, THE ACF GEARS UP FOR FIRST POSTELECTION CAMPAIGN

Dateline — Washington, DC, February 25, 2013

Despite President Hillary Clinton's well-known displeasure with their work, the American Citizen's Foundation's board of directors voted last December to help mobilize the American people in a legislative lobbying effort if the new president would agree to embrace and submit the Democratic model plan, which polls have consistently shown to be favored by majorities ranging from 55 to 65 percent. The president did not endorse the plan as a candidate — a potential sticking point for the ACF — but the public's clear endorsement of her in the election, plus its sustained poll-tested support for the Democratic plan, led a majority of the ACF leadership to conclude that the offer to Clinton was the best way to serve its mission. Spokesperson Olympia Snowe said most board members believed that their action kept alive the possibility that healthcare legislation endorsed by the public could be enacted in this session of Congress.

President Clinton had pledged as a candidate to submit her own plan after her election, and there are indications that in the weeks before the election her pollster, Stanley B. Greenberg, quietly researched the current state of public support for a single-payer healthcare plan similar to the Canadian system. Clinton and her husband had considered and rejected the single payer plan prior to settling on the managed care scheme he submitted to Congress in 1993. Even though the single-payer plan enjoyed significant support among the public and more than a third of congressional Democrats at the time, the first President Clinton avoided it because it relied on large tax increases and regulatory approaches inconsistent with his market-oriented New Democrat philosophy. Since that time, however, problems of access and cost have increased exponentially. Although the ACF policy seminars held in 2011 before the announcement of the Republican and Democratic model plans had considered and rejected the single-payer idea as still not viable politically, President Hillary Clinton was drawn to the idea of a bold surprise proposal that would reflect her values, represent a truly comprehensive solution to the healthcare problem, and establish her as an independent leader.

She was ultimately dissuaded from such a move by three developments: the unexpected retention of congressional control by the Republicans; Greenberg's finding that after months of ACF advertising the model Democratic plan had much greater support than a still-hypothetical single-payer proposal; and the fact that, with the help and encouragement of her defeated opponent, former president Jeb Bush, Republican congressional leaders might well muster enough votes to pass the Republican model healthcare plan despite the well-documented lack of public enthusiasm.

Clinton's decision to scrap the single-payer proposal left her to confront a Republican Congress that could scrape together enough votes to pass its healthcare bill but not to override a presidential veto. That, plus the ACF offer to help her pass the model Democratic proposal if she would endorse it, presented her with an interesting choice. She could be content with the negative political victory that would result from a congressional failure to override her veto of the Republican healthcare voucher plan, or she could embrace the model Democratic proposal and the ACF lobbying help that came with it. In the end, she swallowed her pride and opted for the chance of a positive achievement.

Once the president had accepted its offer, the ACF board had to confront a small political identity crisis of its own, stemming from the fact that some Republican board members, faced with the reality of what they had committed to, were uncomfortable with the idea of working against their friends and former colleagues in Congress on what was, after all, a Democratic Party healthcare bill. After much discussion, it was affirmed that a major purpose of the ACF experiment was precisely to showcase opposition partisans working together to enact the majority will of the people, once it had been clearly expressed. Except in cases like the 2009 Social Security measure, which involved a postelection bipartisan compromise with no direct ACF involvement, it was likely that board members from both parties would eventually find themselves pressing the opposition's agenda in deference to public preferences. Plans were made to have the six Republican board members emphasize this principle in one of the television ads that would be used in the campaign to enlist voters as congressional lobbyists for the winning plan.

The outcome of what will be the first ACF venture into postelection lobbying was impossible to forecast. The prospects were for a pitched battle, with many of the same interests that had so effectively opposed the 1993 Clinton healthcare plan vowing to engage once more in a war for public opinion with the second Clinton administration. On the personal side, this new contest, whose outcome may not be clear for months due to Republican control of the congressional calendar, gave President Hillary Clinton and former President Bill Clinton a unique opportunity to reverse what had been a humiliating defeat for both. Mrs. Clinton was well aware that Harry and Louise could win again unless all available tools, including the ACF, were pressed into service.

As the Clinton administration geared up to push the Medicaid extension plan through Congress, it remained to be seen how they would coordinate their efforts with ACF. It was also uncertain what, if any, role former President Bill Clinton, who has no official position in his wife's administration, might play in the effort. What was clear, however, was that despite the twists and turns of presidential politics and the uncertainty of the outcome, the ACF had managed once again to get a hearing it might not otherwise have gotten for an issue that is of great importance to the public, and to position the voters to act as lobbyists on behalf of a president committed to legislating health care in the name of the people.

Conclusion

We bring the story to a close before we know the outcome to make the following point: significant ACF-bolstered voter influence has already been exerted. The value of its intervention does not depend entirely on whether the fictional Clinton/AFC/public partnership ends in victory or compromise legislation, optimal though that would be. If there were another meltdown, it would simply mean that Congress found ways to resist the pressure, which is always a possibility. Nevertheless, ACF efforts would still have strengthened the public hand in the policy debate in several important ways. It would still have reached the people with a clear explanation of the problem, and it would have intensified the public's already strong conviction that the problem deserved the attention of the presidential candidates. That combination would still have made the problem a campaign issue the candidates could not ignore, whether or not they agreed to pledge support for a model option. If the winning candidate did sign on to the voters' policy choice, ACF would have voters poised to try their hand at direct congressional lobbying. What is more, all these things would have been orchestrated without abridging any candidate freedom except the freedom to ignore a problem that the voters want addressed.

The contrast between the electoral leverage available to this imaginary election winner and the lack of the same behind the Clinton healthcare proposal of 1993–1994 could not be more striking. In those years, nobody supportive of the Clinton plan extensively briefed the voters or asked for their help in Congress. Instead, President Clinton largely conceded the fight for public opinion to his opponents, who mobilized their own partnership with the public, based on misinformation and fear. The debate over health care was thus shaped not by a real choice between two well-crafted options but by a false choice between a demonized plan on the one hand and inaction on the other.

Note   1. References for the healthcare scenario include Toner (2003); Brock (2003a); Issues for Debate in American Public Policy (2000); Jacobs and Shapiro (2000), Pauly and Herring (2001); and Feder et al. (2001).

References

Aitken, Jonathan. 1993. *Nixon: A Life.* Washington, D.C.: Regnery Publishing, Inc.

Ambrose, Stephen E. 1989. *Nixon: The Triumph of a Politician 1962–1972.* Vol. Two. New York: Simon and Schuster.

Baker, Dean, and Mark Weisbrot. 1999. *Social Security: The Phony Crisis.* Chicago: University of Chicago Press.

Bark, Ed. 1996. "Presidential Debate Draws Record Low Ratings Nationwide." *Dallas Morning News,* September 10, p. 20A.

Barone, Michael. 2001. *The Almanac of American Politics.* Washington, D.C.: National Journal.

Barta, Carolyn. 1993. *Perot and His People.* Fort Worth, Tex.: The Summit Group.

Bartels, Larry M., and Lynn Vavreck, eds. 2000. *Campaign Reform.* Ann Arbor: The University of Michigan Press.

Bennet, James. 1998. "Justice Department Questions President in '96 Campaign Finance Inquiry." *New York Times,* November 10, p. A1.

Berke, Richard L. 1996. "Clinton and Dole, Face to Face, Spar over Medicare and Taxes." *New York Times,* October 7, p. A1.

Berke, Richard L., and Janet Elder. 2001. *New York Times,* June 21, p. A1.

Big Choices: The Future of Health Insurance for America's Families. 2003. Conference hosted by the Lyndon Baines Johnson Library and Museum and the Center for Health and Social Policy, Lyndon B. Johnson School of Public Affairs, University of Texas at Austin. April 25.

Birnbaum, Jeffry H., and Michael K. Frisby. 1992. "Clinton Puts Emphasis on Deficit Goal as He Maps His Economic Plan." *Wall Street Journal,* December 18, p. A1.

Bornet, Vaughn Davis. 1983. *The Presidency of Lyndon B. Johnson.* Lawrence: University Press of Kansas.

Brock, Fred. 2003a. "Why a Centrist (No Fooling) Wants Universal Insurance." *New York Times,* January 5, section 3, p. 7.

———.2003b. "Lost in the Shuffle, a Sign of Strength for Social Security." *New York Times,* April 13, section 3, p. 8.

Broder, David. 1999. "Opportunity for Social Security Reforms Going, Going...." *Austin American-Statesman,* April 28, p. A17.

Brody, Richard A. 1991. *Assessing the President.* Stanford, Calif.: Stanford University Press.

Bruni, Frank. 2001. "Where George Bush Leads, Who Will Follow?" *New York Times,* February 25, section 4, p. 16.

———.2002. Ambling into History: The Unlikely Odyssey of George W. Bush. New York: Harper-Collins.

Buchanan, Bruce. 1987. *The Citizen's Presidency.* Washington, D.C.: Congressional Quarterly Press.

———.1988. The New Presidential Leadership Agenda. Paper presented at the annual meeting of the American Political Science Association, September, Washington, D.C.

———.1991. *Electing a President: The Markle Commission Research on Campaign '88*. Austin: University of Texas Press.

———.1995. "A Tale of Two Campaigns." *Political Psychology* 16: 297–319.

———.1996. *Renewing Presidential Politics: Campaigns, Media, and the Public Interest*. Lanham, Md: Rowman and Littlefield.

———.1999a. "Presidential Campaign Quality: What the Variance Implies." *Presidential Studies Quarterly* 29: 798–819.

———.1999b. Presidential Candidates, Voter Incentives, and Campaign Reform. Paper presented at the annual meeting of the American Political Science Association, September, Washington, D.C.

———.2001. Participation and Policy in Presidential Elections: A Typology of Voter Influence. Paper presented at the annual meeting of the American Political Science Association, September, San Francisco.

———.2002. Presidents, Publics, and Policy Partnerships. Paper presented at the annual meeting of the American Political Science Association, Boston, August 31–September 3.

———.2004. *Presidential Campaign Quality: Incentives and Reform*. Upper Saddle River, N.J.: Prentice-Hall.

Burnham, Walter Dean. 1970. *Critical Elections and the Mainsprings of American Electoral Politics*. New York: Norton.

Bush, George H. W. 1998. Personal communication, October 1.

Calmes, Jackie. 2001. "Public Buys Tax-Cut Plan Sold by Bush." *Wall Street Journal*, March 8, p. A9.

Cameron, Charles M. 2002. "Studying the Polarized Presidency." *Presidential Studies Quarterly*, 32: 647–663.

Campaign '96 R.I.P. 1996. *New York Times*, November 3, section 4, p. 14.

Campbell, Angus, Philip E. Converse, Warren E. Miller, and Donald E. Stokes. 1960. *The American Voter*. New York: Wiley.

Cannon, Lou. 1982. *Reagan*. New York: Putnam.

Ceaser, James, and Andrew Busch. 1993. *Upside Down and Inside Out: The 1992 Elections and American Politics*. Lanham, Md: Rowman and Littlefield.

———. 1997. Losing to Win: The 1996 Elections and American Politics. Lanham, Md: Rowman and Littlefield.

Chubb, John, and Paul Peterson, eds. 1985. *The New Direction in American Politics*. Washingson, D.C.: Brookings.

Clymer, Adam. 1993. "Poll Takers Say It Was the Economy, Stupid." *New York Times*, May 24, p. A12.

———. 1996. "G.O.P. Pushes Congress Strategy That Shuns Dole." *New York Times*, October 23, p. A1.

Cohen, Wilbur J. 1986. "Education." Pp. 103–105 in *The Great Society: A Twenty Year Critique*, ed. Barbara C. Jordan and Elspeth Rostow. Austin, Tex.: Lyndon Baines Johnson Library, Lyndon B. Johnson School of Public Affairs.

Conley, Patricia H. 2001. *Presidential Mandates: How Elections Shape the National Agenda*. Chicago: University of Chicago Press.

Cramer, Richard Ben. 1992. *What It Takes*. New York: Random House.

Crockett, David A. 2002. *The Opposition Presidency*. College Station: Texas A&M University Press.

Cronin, Thomas E. 1989. *Direct Democracy: The Politics of Initiative, Referendum and Recall*. Cambridge, Mass.: Harvard University Press.

Dahl, Robert A. 1990. "The Myth of the Presidential Mandate." *Political Science Quarterly*, 105: 355–72.

———. 1998. *On Democracy*. New Haven, Conn.: Yale University Press.

Dallek, Robert. 1998. *Flawed Giant: Lyndon Johnson and His Times 1961–1973*. New York: Oxford University Press.

Dallek, Robert. 2003. *An Unfinished Life: John F. Kennedy 1917–1963*. Boston, MA: Little, Brown.

Darman, Richard. 1996. "If We Were Serious." *New York Times*, September 1, section 4, p. 9.

"Deficit Politics Returns." 2002. *New York Times*, January 8, p. A22.

Dole, Bob. 1998. "The Election Was Decided by Early 1996." *Wall Street Journal*, January 15, p. A18.

Drew, Elisabeth. 1989. *Election Journal: Political Events of 1987–1988*. New York: William Morrow.

Dye, Thomas R. 2001. *Top Down Policymaking.* New York: Chatham House.

Edwards, George C. III. 1990. *Presidential Approval: A Sourcebook.* Baltimore, Md: Johns Hopkins University Press.

———. Forthcoming. *On Deaf Ears:The Limits of the Bully Pulpit.* New Haven, Conn.: Yale University Press.

Executive Summary. 1998. *Report to the Markle Foundation: Media Coverage of Campaign '96.* Washington, D.C.: Center for Media and Public Affairs.

Feder, Judith, Larry Levitt, Ellen O'Brien, and Diane Rowland. 2001. "Covering the Low-Income Uninsured: The Case for Expanding Public Programs." *Health Affairs*, January–February: 27–39.

Feinsilber, Michael. 1992. "Battling Booklets by Bush, Clinton." *Austin American-Statesman*, September 13, p. A14.

Fiorina, Morris P., and Paul E. Peterson. 1998. *The New American Democracy.* Needham Heights, Mass.: Allyn and Bacon.

Fishel, Jeff. 1985. *Presidents and Promises: From Campaign Pledge to Presidential Performance.* Washington, D.C.: Congressional Quarterly Press.

Fishkin, James. 1995. *The Voice of the People: Democracy and Public Opinion.* New Haven, Conn.: Yale University Press.

Gallup, George H. 1972. *The Gallup Poll: 1935–1971.* New York: Random House.

Gallup Poll Archives. June 1964–October 1965. "Most Important Problem." Question ID numbers US Gallup.694.Q001–717.Q004A.

———. March 18, 1965. "Most Important Problem." Question ID number USGallup.706.Q003A.

———. March 1980–October 1981. "Most Important Problem." Question ID numbers USGallup.1151.Q02A–1183.Q002A.

Gallup Poll News Service. May 17, 2001. "Surge in Public's View of Energy as Great Problem." *Wysiwyg://7/http://gallup.com/Poll/releases/pr010517b.asp*

Gans, Curtiss B. Personal communication, February 2001.

Germond, Jack W., and Jules Whitcover. 1989. Whose Broad Stripes and Bright Stars? The Trivial Pursuit of the Presidency 1988. New York: Warner Books.

Giglio, James N. 1991. *The Presidency of John F. Kennedy.* Lawrence: University Press of Kansas.

Ginsberg, Benjamin. 1976. "Elections and Public Policy." *The American Political Science Review*, March: 41–49.

Goldman, Keven. 1995. "TV Will Be a Winner in the '96 Elections." *Wall Street Journal*, July 14, p. B8.

Goldman, Peter. 1981. "The Reagan Steamroller." *Newsweek*, May 18, p. 40.

Goldman, Peter, and Tom Mathews. 1989. *The Quest for the Presidency: The 1988 Campaign.* New York: Simon and Schuster.

Gordon, Colin. 2003. *Dead on Arrival: The Politics of Health Care in Twentieth-Century America.* Princeton, N.J.: Princeton University Press.

Gould, Lewis L. 1993. *1968: The Election That Changed America.* Chicago: Ivan R. Dee.

———. 2003. *The Modern American Presidency.* Lawrence: University Press of Kansas.

Graham, Hugh Davis. 1981. "The Transformation of Federal Education Policy." In *Exploring the Johnson Years*, ed. Robert A. Divine. Austin: University of Texas Press, pp. 155–184.

Greene, John Robert. 2000. *The Presidency of George Bush.* Lawrence: University Press of Kansas.

Greenfield, Jeff. 1995. "Powell Can Win." *New York Times*, October 9, p. A11.

Greenstein, Fred I., ed. 1983. *The Reagan Presidency: An Early Assessment.* Baltimore, Md: Johns Hopkins University Press.

———. 2000. The Presidential Difference: Leadership Style from FDR to Clinton. New York: Free Press.

Gutmann, Amy, and Dennis Thompson. 1996. *Democracy and Disagreement.* Cambridge, Mass.: Belknap Press of Harvard University Press.

Hacker, Jacob. 1997. *The Road to Nowhere: The Genesis of President Clinton's Plan for Health Security.* Princeton, N.J.: Princeton University Press.

Harwood, John. 2003a. "Gephardt Offers Health-Care Plan with Hefty Price." *Wall Street Journal*, April 24, p. A4.

———. 2003b. "Democratic Rivals' Health-Care Plans Target Primary Voters." *Wall Street Journal*, May 21, p. A4.

———. 2003c. "Tax-Cut Victory May Prove Costly for Bush." *Wall Street Journal*, May 22, p. A4.

Held, David. 1996. *Models of Democracy.* 2d ed. Stanford, Calif.: Stanford University Press.

Hawkins, Augustus. 1986. "Statement on Education and Health." In *Exploring the Johnson Years,* ed. Robert A. Divine. Austin: University of Texas Press, pp. 105–108.

Holmes, Steven A. 1992. "Bold Perot Plan to Attack Deficit Thrusts Issue at Bush and Clinton." *New York Times,* September 28, p. A1.

Hume, Ellen. 1990. "Why the Press Blew the S&L Scandal." *New York Times,* May 24, p. A25.

Huntington, Samuel P. 1991. *The Third Wave: Democratization in the Late Twentieth Century.* Norman: University of Oklahoma Press.

Issues for Debate in American Public Policy. 2d ed. 2000. *Selections from the CQ Researcher.* Washington, D.C.: Congressional Quarterly Press.

Iyengar, Shanto. 1991. *Is Anyone Responsible? How Television Frames Political Issues.* Chicago: University of Chicago Press.

Jacobs, Lawrence R., and Robert Y. Shapiro. 1992. Public Decisions, Private Polls: John F. Kennedy's Presidency. Paper presented at the annual meeting of the Midwest Political Science Association, September, Chicago.

———. 2000. *Politicians Don't Pander: Political Manipulation and the Loss of Democratic Responsiveness.* Chicago: University of Chicago Press.

Jamieson, Kathleen Hall. 1988. "Is Truth Now Irrelevant in Presidential Campaigns?" *Washington Post National Weekly Edition,* November 7–13, p. 28.

Johnson, Dennis W. 2001. No Place for Amateurs: How Political Consultants Are Reshaping American Democracy. New York: Routledge.

Johnson, Haynes, and David S. Broder. 1996. *The System.* Boston: Little, Brown.

Jones, Charles O. 1988. *The Trusteeship Presidency: Jimmy Carter and the United States Congress.* Baton Rouge: Louisiana State University Press.

———. *The Presidency in a Separated System.* Washington, D.C.: Brookings.

Jost, Kenneth. 2000. "Patients' Rights." Pp. 41–59 in *Issues for Debate in American Public Policy.* 2d ed. Washington, D.C.: Congressional Quarterly Press.

Jordan, Barbara C., and Elspeth D. Rostow, eds. 1986. *The Great Society: A Twenty Year Critique.* Austin, Tex.: Lyndon B. Johnson Library and School of Public Affairs.

Kaufman, Burton I. 1993. *The Presidency of James Earl Carter.* Lawrence: University Press of Kansas.

Kelley, Stanley, Jr. 1983. *Interpreting Elections.* Princeton, N.J.: Princeton University Press.

Kernell, Samuel. 1997. *Going Public: New Strategies of Presidential Leadership.* Washington, D.C.: Congressional Quarterly Press.

Key, V. O. 1955. "A Theory of Critical Elections." *Journal of Politics* 17: 3–18.

Klein, Joe. 2002. The Natural: The Misunderstood Presidency of Bill Clinton. New York: Doubleday.

Lemann, Nicholas. 2003. "The Controller." *The New Yorker,* May 12, p. 68.

Lewis, Neil A. 2003. "Stymied by Democrats in Senate, Bush Court Pick Finally Gives Up." *New York Times,* September 5, p. A1.

Liebovich, Louis W. 2001. *The Press and the Modern Presidency: Myths and Mindsets from Kennedy to Election 2000.* rev. ed. Westport, Conn.: Praeger.

Lipman, Larry. 2003. "Health Care is Dominant Issue for Democrats." *Austin American-Statesman,* September 21, p. A17.

Lueck, Sarah. 2003. "Physicians Group Advocates Medical Coverage for All in U.S." *Wall Street Journal,* August 13, p. D2.

Marmor, Theodore, ed. 1994. *Understanding Health Care Reform.* New Haven, Conn.: Yale University Press.

McPherson, Harry. 1972. *A Political Education.* Boston: Little, Brown.

Miller, William Lee. 2002. *Lincoln's Virtues: An Ethical Biography.* New York: Knopf.

Mitchell, Andrea, "After the Nicknames," March 9, 2001. *New York Times,* p A12.

Morris, Dick. 1997. *Behind the Oval Office.* New York: Random House.

Murray, Alan. 1991. "Economy in the U.S. Isn't Nearly as Sour as the Country's Mood." *Wall Street Journal,* November 4, p. A1.

———. 1992. "The Fiscal Proposals of Bush and Clinton Both Flunk Arithmetic." *Wall Street Journal,* September 15, p. A1.

Nagourney, Adam. 1996. "The Year of the Yawn." *New York Times,* November 3, section 4, p. 1.

———. 2003a. "Gephardt Issues Proposal on Health Insurance." *New York Times*, April 24, p. A26.

———. 2003b. "Preparing for Democratic Contenders' Forum in Des Moines, Kerry Issues Health Plan." *New York Times*, May 17, p. A12.

Nagourney, Adam, and Janet Elder. 2003. "Bush's Support Strong Despite Tax Cut Doubts." *New York Times*, May 14, p. A1.

Neustadt, Richard. 1990. Presidential Power and the Modern Presidents: The Politics of Leadership from Roosevelt to Reagan. New York: Free Press.

Nixon, Richard M. 1962. *Six Crises*. New York: Pyramid Books.

———. 1978. *RN: The Memoirs of Richard Nixon*. New York: Grosset and Dunlap.

Ornstein, Norman J., and Mark Schmitt. 1989. "The 1988 Election." *Foreign Affairs* 68: 39–52.

Pach, Chester J., and Elmo Richardson. 1991. *The Presidency of Dwight D. Eisenhower*. rev. ed. Lawrence: University Press of Kansas.

Page, Benjamin I., and Robert Y. Shapiro. 1992. *The Rational Public: Fifty Years of Trends in Americans' Policy Preferences*. Chicago: University of Chicago Press.

Palmer, John L., and Isabel V. Sawhill, eds. 1984. *The Reagan Record*. Cambridge, Mass.: Ballinger Publishing Company.

Patterson, James T. 1996. Grand Expectations: The United States, 1945–1974. New York: Oxford University Press.

Patterson, Thomas E. 2002. The Vanishing Voter: Public Involvement in an Age of Uncertainty. New York: Knopf.

Pauly, M., and B. Herring. 2001. "Expanding Insurance Coverage through Tax Credits: Tradeoffs and Options." *Health Affairs* January–February: 1–18.

Pear, Robert. 2003a. "New Study Finds 60 Million Uninsured during a Year." *New York Times*, May 13, p. A20.

———. 2003b. "Bush Drug Proposal in Medicare Plan Faces a Stiff Battle." *New York Times*, May 21, p. A1.

Pereira, Joe. 2003. "Canada's Health-Care System Offers Cost Savings, Study Finds." *Wall Street Journal*, August 21, p. D3.

Perret, Geoffrey. 2001. *Jack: A Life Like No Other.* New York: Random House.

Peterson, Peter G. 2003. "Deficits and Dysfunction: How the Republicans (and Democrats) Have Sold Out Our Future." *New York Times Magazine*, June 8, p. 15.

Pew Research Center for the People and the Press News Release. 2003. *Bush Approval Slips — Fix Economy Say Voters*. August 7. Washington, D.C.: Pew Research Center.

Pew Online Reports. 2001. "Bush Approval on Par, No Tax Cut Momentum." February. http://www.people-press.org/feb01rpt.htm.

Pew Research Center for the People and the Press News Release. 2000. *Bush Gains on Personal Qualities*. November 1. Washington, D.C.: Pew Research Center.

Polling Report.com.2003. Problems and Priorities. http://www.pollingreport.com.prioriti.htm.

Polman, Dick. 2003. "Democratic Hopefuls Focus on Health Care." *Austin American-Statesman*, May 18, p. A11.

Pool, Ithiel de Sola, Robert P. Abelson, and Samuel L. Popkin. 1964. *Candidates, Issues, and Strategies: A Computer Simulation of the 1960 and 1964 Presidential Elections.* Cambridge, Mass.: The M.I.T. Press.

Princeton Survey Research Associates. 1997. *Report to the Markle Foundation*. Princeton, N.J.: Princeton Survey Research Associates.

Putnam, Robert D. 2000. Bowling Alone: The Collapse and Revival of American Community. New York: Simon & Schuster.

Ragsdale, Lyn, and Jerrold G. Rusk. 1999. "Elections and Presidential Policymaking." Pp. 98–116 in *Presidential Policymaking: An End-of-Century Assessment*, ed. Steven A. Shull. Armonk, N.Y.: M.E. Sharp.

Reeves, Richard. 1993. *President Kennedy: Profile of Power*. New York: Simon and Schuster.

———. 2001. *President Nixon: Alone in the White House*. New York: Simon and Schuster.

Roberts, Steven V. 1982. "President's Coalition." *New York Times,* October 27, p. 13.

Rom, Mark. 1996. *Public Spirit in the Thrift Tragedy*. Pittsburgh: University of Pittsburgh Press.

Roper Center Public Opinion Online. 1989a. "Gallup Poll: What Things Do You Like Best About President Johnson?" January 28–February 2, 1965. Accession Number 0039542.

————. 1989b. "Gallup Poll: States or Federal Government Pay Increased Education Costs?" January 28–February 2, 1965. Accession Number 0039566.

————. 1989c. "ABC News/*Washington Post* Poll: Reagan Tax and Budget Cut Approval." February 19–20, 1981. Accession Numbers 0006883; 0006881.

————. 1989d. "ABC News/*Washington Post* Poll: Reagan Tax and Budget Cut Approval." March 25–29, 1981. Accession Numbers 0007231;0007229.

————. 1989e. "ABC News/*Washington Post* Poll: Reagan Budget Cut Approval." April 20–22, 1981. Accession Number 0007401.

————. 1989f. "NBC News/Associate Press Poll: Reagan Tax Cut Approval." May 18–19, 1981. Accession Number 0084811.

————. 1989g. "Gallup Poll: Spending Cuts About Right/Too Low." May 8–11,1981. Accession Number 0029696.

————. 1989h. "Gallup Poll: Reagan Tax Cut Approval." August 14–17, 1981. Accession Number 0029899.

————. 1990. "Gallup Poll: Satisfaction with Public School System." February, 1965. Accession Number 0038892.

————. 1995. "Louis Harris and Associates: Favor Johnson on Federal Aid to Education?" April, 1965. Accession Number 0245688.

————. 2001. "ABC News/*Washington Post* Poll: Tax Cut or Spending?" May 31–June 3. Accession Number 0382712.

Rosenstone, Steven J., Roy L. Behr, and Edward H. Lazarus. 1996. *Third Parties in America.* 2nd ed. Princeton, N.J.: Princeton University Press.

Rosenthal, A.M. 1995. "The Powell Point." *New York Times*, November 10, p. A17.

Sanger, David E. 2001. "President's Signature Turns Broad Tax Cut, and a Campaign Promise, into Law." *New York Times*, June 8, p. A8.

Sanger, David E., and Marc Lacey. 2001. "In Early Battles, Bush Learns Need for Compromises." *New York Times*, April 29, p. 1.

Schattschneider, Elmer E. 1960. *The Semisovereign People: A Realist's View of Democracy in America.* New York: Holt, Rinehart, and Winston.

Schlesinger, Jacob M., and Laura Heinauer. 2001. "Well-to-Do Gain Most in Bush Tax Plan." *Wall Street Journal*, February 7, p. A28.

Schumpeter, Joseph A. 1976. *Capitalism, Socialism and Democracy.* New York: Harper and Row.

Shafer, Ronald G. 1996. "Washington Wire." *Wall Street Journal*, October 25, p. A1.

Shapiro, Ian. 2003. *The State of Democratic Theory.* Princeton, N.J.: Princeton University Press.

Shapiro, Robert Y., and Lawrence R. Jacobs. 2000. Presidents and Polling: Politicians, Pandering, and the Study of Democratic Responsiveness. Paper presented at the annual meeting of the American Political Science Association, Washington, D.C., August 30–September 3.

Shribman, D., and T. Noah. 1992. "Perot's Decision to Run Scrambles Campaign, May Help Bush a Bit." *Wall Street Journal,* October 2, A1.

Shuman, Howard E. 1992. *Politics and the Budget.* 3d ed. Engelwood Cliffs, N.J.: Prentice-Hall.

Skocpol, Theda. 1997. Boomerang: Clinton's Health Security Effort and the Turn against Government in the U.S. New York: Norton.

Sorensen, Theodore C. 1965. *Kennedy.* New York: Harper and Row.

Stahl, Lori. 1996. "Perot Complains to FCC about Ad Time." *Dallas Morning News*, September 25, p. A-6.

Stevenson, Richard W. 2001a. "In Policy Change, Greenspan Backs a Broad Tax Cut." *New York Times*, January 26, p. A1.

————. 2001b. "President Unveils $1.96 Trillion Plan That Trims Taxes." *New York Times*, March 1, p. A1

————. 2001c. "Victory in Defeat." *New York Times*, April 7, p. A9.

————. 2001d. "Congress Passes Tax Cut, with Rebates This Summer." *New York Times*, May 27, p. A1.

————. 2003. "Candidate Bush Files Papers for '04 Race." *New York Times*, May 17, p. A12.

Stockman, David A. 1986. *The Triumph of Politics: How the Reagan Revolution Failed.* New York: Harper and Row.

Strom, Stephanie. 2003. "Foundations Roiled by Measure to Spur Increase in Charity." *New York Times*, May 19, p. A1.

Sundquist, James L. 1983. *Dynamics of the Party System.* rev. ed. Washington, D. C.: Brookings.

Taylor, Paul. 1988. "The Bush-Dukakis Pact: Mum's the Word on the Deficit." *Washington Post National Weekly Edition*, May 30–June 5.

———. 1989. "Pigsty Politics: The 1988 Presidential Race Set a New Standard for Negative Ads." *Washington Post National Weekly Edition*, February 13–19, p. 7.

Taylor, Paul, and David S. Broder. 1988. "How the Presidential Campaign Got Stuck on the Low Road." *Washington Post National Weekly Edition,* November 7–13, p. 14.

Toedtman, James, and Elaine S. Povich. 2001. "Bush Hoping Trip Boosts Tax Plan." *Newsday,* March 11, p. A19.

Toner, Robin. 1992. "Political Metamorphoses: Voters Impose Discipline on the Candidates as Perot Finds a New Way of Campaigning." *New York Times,* November 3, p. A1.

———. 2003. "Medicare: Battleground for a Bigger Struggle." *New York Times*, July 20, section 4 p. 12

Troy, Gil. 1991. *See How They Ran*. New York: Free Press.

Waugh, John C. 1997. Reelecting Lincoln: The Battle for the 1864 Presidency. New York: Crown.

Weisman, Jonathan. 2001. "Bush's Tax Cut Hardball." *USA Today*, May 29, p. 8A.

Wessel, David, and Jeffrey H. Birnbaum. 1992. "Clinton Advisers Find Promises Are Easier to Make Than Keep." *Wall Street Journal*, November 19, p. A1.

White, Theodore H. 1982. America in Search of Itself: The Making of the President 1956–1980. New York: Harper and Row.

Wilson Center News Digest. 2002. Committee Leadership in Congress, February 8. http://wwics.si.edu/NEWS/digest/comldrshp.htm.

Witcover, Jules. 2001. No Way to Pick a President: How Money and Hired Guns Have Debased American Elections. New York: Routledge.

Woodward, Bob. 1994. *The Agenda: Inside the Clinton White House*. New York: Simon and Schuster.

Wynn, Kelli. 2003. "Doctors Push for Federally Financed Insurance." *Austin American-Statesman*, August 13, p. A6.

Zaller, John R. 1992. *The Nature and Origins of Mass Opinion.* New York: Cambridge University Press.

Index